HAUNTED DERBY
Myths, Magic and Folklore

HAUNTED DERBY
Myths, Magic and Folklore

Wayne Anthony and Jude Savage

DB PUBLISHING

First published in Great Britain in 2007 by
The Breedon Books Publishing Company Limited
Breedon House, 3 The Parker Centre,
Derby, DE21 4SZ.

This paperback edition published in Great Britain in 2014 by DB Publishing,
an imprint of JMD Media Ltd

Wayne Anthony

Wayne Anthony descends from a long line of practicing psychics and mediums. Having been raised in an environment where unusual psychic phenomena were an everyday occurrence he decided to write about the subject at an early age. He is the author of numerous books on ghosts and the supernatural, three of which are on Derbyshire and the Peak District. Having appeared on national and international television and radio he is recognised as a leading authority in this field and is frequently consulted for his expertise. He has also written extensively for newspapers and magazines and is working on his first supernatural thriller.

BA (Hons) Theatre Arts

Jude Savage

Jude Savage was raised in Derbyshire and has been fascinated by the rich tapestry of myths and legends of this shire since childhood. Her interests in ghosts and the supernatural occurred as a direct result of coming face to face with something 'other-worldly' on a dark country road over a decade ago. Having researched the subject extensively she is now pursuing a career in writing. As part of her Theatre Arts Honorary Degree she has studied anthropological aspects of Elizabethan folklore and magic.

ISBN 978-1-78091-422-0

Printed and bound in Great Britain by Marston Book Services Ltd, Oxfordshire

Contents

Acknowledgements   6

Introduction   7

Preface   9

Telltale Signs of the Dead   11

City of the Dead   13

Hours of the Living   45

Supernature   68

The Worlds Within   98

Merry Spirits   117

Wraith of Shades   127

Don't Look Back   149

Lexicon Mystique   169

Bibliography   192

Acknowledgements

The authors would like to thank all the people who have so willingly opened their hearts, homes, personal histories, and allowed us to trample on their lands and take intrusive photographs while the research for this book was under way. A special thank you is due to the people of Derby and Derbyshire, who have so willingly contributed little-known facts about the culture and heritage of their beloved shire.

The authors are particularly grateful to their families and friends for their support, understanding and encouragement while the book was being written. Special thanks are due to Sir Geoffrey Rhadlon, for the idea to write about ghosts in the first place; Sarah Powlson, for making us look good; *The Derby Evening Telegraph, The Derby Express, The Derby Trader, The Derbyshire, Nottinghamshire* and *Leicestershire Now Magazines* for their help in highlighting Derbyshire as one of the counties most rich in ancient legends and folklore.

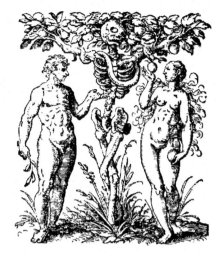

Introduction

What is a ghost? A terrible event condemned to repeat itself time and time again? An instant of pain perhaps, caught within its own eternity? An unhappy spirit, which, like William Shakespeare stated in *Hamlet*, is 'doomed for a certain term to walk the night, and for the day confined to fast in fires', or maybe these creatures of half light and half darkness are mere recordings of twisted events long since past. The unhappy dead, wraiths that exist within the shadows lamenting their untimely departure, cursing their outcast state, frozen within their unhappiness? Are they waiting for such a time to arrive that they may reveal themselves to the living for reasons best known to themselves? To gain absolution perhaps? To be forgiven for their terrible crimes? To reveal their tragedy to the world, thus enabling them to be released from their trapped state – like an insect caught within amber? Maybe all of these things – maybe none of these things – for who can really say?

One thing is for sure, ghosts are being seen in and around Derby and its shire nearly every day of the week. But why is it that Derby and the Peak District have so many sightings of ghosts? There appear to be many reasons, but perhaps the two most obvious ones are that the region has been a major crossing point for many cultures, from the Beaker peoples, Saxons, Vikings and the Romans, right through to modern-day man. Secondly, it is an area of Britain furthest from the beautiful seas that surround it, a hilly terrain where, in ancient times, very little immigration or emigration took place. The people that decided to stay kept with them a rich tapestry of folklore, magic, and superstitions as well as their pagan traditions that are now all but forgotten by today's society. Some, however, have been retained and we need only to delve into the great history of this country to begin to find them. Tales of myths and legends, sorcery and dark magic, natural and the supernatural, nature and supernature, other-worldly beings and even extraterrestrial visitors.

It is hoped that the reader will find a wide variety of some of the more unusual aspects of our heritage within these pages and perhaps some of these stories will enable us to take a different look at our ancestry, age-old customs and practices that we so often take for granted.

The stories that are to be found in this book are in no way necessarily my opinion. They are merely accounts of other people's experiences and beliefs, as well as an historical look at some of the anthropological aspects of human belief systems, presented here in the hope that we may re-evaluate our stance on the paranormal. The book is not meant to make people 'change' their opinions, but instead to encourage them to accept that folklore and superstition are as much part of our culture and heritage today as they ever were. It is these things that give any culture a dimension of quality and a depth of soul.

Whenever I am asked what a ghost is I find it difficult to reply with any certainty. I prefer, instead, to point people in the direction of personal research so that they can unravel for themselves exactly what a ghost is. Or, at the very least, they can begin to ascertain for themselves what a ghost might be. One thing is for sure, ghosts are real – so many people see so many odd things. Personally, I don't come from the school of thought that says people are easily duped by their own imaginations; I think humans should be given more credit then that. I often hear the words 'Well I've never EVER seen anything'; to which my reply is that people are more or less sensitive to seeing ghosts – those that do not and have never seen them are thus surely among the less sensitive.

So, what is a ghost? Let us immerse ourselves in the following pages and attempt to find out…

Wayne Anthony
Spring 2007

Preface

On one cold, clear, starry night in November, I was driving home along a country road in Derbyshire with a friend. We had been out for the evening and, as it was approximately two in the morning, the roads were clear as we made our way home. Despite the lateness of the hour, we were both feeling wide-awake and chatted happily as I wove the car through the bends of the country lanes, my lights on full beam wherever possible due to the lack of street lamps.

Suddenly, as I was approaching a bend in the lane, I noticed what appeared to be an isolated cloud of smoke or patch of fog in the middle of the road ahead. As the car drew closer, to my horror I saw that the smoke or fog formed the shape of an old woman with long, flowing hair. As a natural reaction, I swerved the car slightly to try and avoid whatever it was. In doing so, however, the figure seemed to come through the car itself, reaching forwards through the windscreen.

Although I wasn't travelling particularly fast, the whole incident seemed to happen in an instant and I immediately exclaimed 'What on earth was that?' To my surprise, my friend replied with 'That was a woman; she was quite tall wasn't she?' He went on to provide, without me having uttered another word, a full description of her. At this point I knew we had witnessed the same thing, and, with mounting dread, I began to feel that our experience was other-worldly.

As we continued our journey we tried to come to some logical explanation for what had just happened. I like to think we are both quite rational, down-to-earth people, not prone to flights of fancy, and we decided that there must be some sensible explanation. However, we could not seem to find one. The weather was dry and clear that night, and we had encountered no other patches of fog during our journey. We also concluded that what we had seen could not be smoke, because it had formed an isolated and dense shape, rather than drifting straight upwards.

Had it not been for the fact that my friend had given a description of the 'woman' which corresponded exactly with the image in my mind, I would have put the experience down to a figment of my imagination.

Did we experience something supernatural? Did we, dare I say it, see a ghost? Or, is there a perfectly logical explanation for what happened?

I'm sure many of the people of Derby who have had similar experiences have asked themselves the same questions. The number of people witness to such occurrences within Derby, which has been nicknamed 'the Ghost Capital of England', is abundant.

This book incorporates many of these strange encounters, kindly told to us by the people of Derby, presented among these pages not to prove or disprove such phenomena exist, but merely to provide the accounts of people who feel they have experienced something of the paranormal. Many readers will argue that logical explanations can be found for every 'ghostly encounter' listed here, but perhaps these readers would remain sceptical even if they experienced something similar themselves?

The book also delves into the rich tapestry of folklore associated with this shire; it explores the myths, magic and legends which have been passed down the generations to the people of Derby.

Whatever your beliefs, we simply invite you to read these pages and make up your own minds, hopefully discovering along the way that Derby has more dark secrets and hidden stories beneath its surface than you ever imagined.

Jude Savage
Spring 2007

Telltale Signs of the Dead

Is There a Ghost in Your House?

The 12 Key Signs that Could Indicate a Ghost in your House.

1. You hear unexplained and strange noises.

2. Lights go on and off of their own accord.

3. Electrical equipment continually breaks down.

4. You cannot sleep or wake up in the early hours of the morning with feelings of 'not being alone'.

5. Items are inexplicably moved around.

6. You see something – shadows, shapes – often out of the corner of your eye.

7. Unusual or horrible smells pervade certain areas of the building at certain times.

8. You regularly feel exhausted and unable to concentrate.

9. You are experiencing icy blasts of air or unusual cold areas within the building, or there are radical temperature changes.

10. There are certain times of the day which don't 'feel right' in your home.

11. You feel very uncomfortable in one particular room in the house.

12. Random scratching noises can be heard coming from different rooms or from beneath the floorboards.

City of the Dead

Allestree

T he Anglo-Saxons settled at Allestree, probably attracted by its south-facing location, the plentiful supply of water and the excellent quality of the soil. They were not the first to inhabit the area, however, as Bronze Age archaeology has been unearthed not far from the village.

It was recorded in the Domesday Book of 1086 that the manor of Markeaton was held by the Earl of Chester. In the middle of the 12th century most of the land was granted and sold to the recently founded Abbey of St Mary at Darley.

Allestree ghost. The figure of a ghostly monk, dressed in a black habit, is seen at the rear of St Edmund's Church and has been spotted near to the iron railings.

St Edmund's Church, Allestree.

In 1516, the manor of Markeaton came into the hands of John Mundy, a goldsmith, who later became the Lord Mayor of London. The Mundy family were anxious to make the most of their acquisition, and, after the break up of the feudal system, new methods of farming, dairy production and crop-growing were experimented with. These changes inevitably raised the standard of living for the villagers.

The Mundy family continued to own the estate until the 1780s, when it was sold to Thomas Evans, a Darley Abbey mill owner. In the middle of the 19th century Bache Thornhill, of Stanton-in-Peak, bought Allestree Park and built a house on the site, although he died before the project was completed. His ghost is said to be seen 'frowning, with a concerned look on his face', inspecting the building.

In 1928, the park was purchased by a firm of builders, who proceeded to build houses on the site. The outbreak of World War Two put an end to this project. During the war the army and then the fire brigade used Allestree Hall, and the fire brigade continued to use the hall until the 1950s. The council then took over the hall and its 323 acres of the park. A nine-hole golf course was installed there in 1948, and was extended to 18 holes in 1955.

In 1868 St Edmund's stopped being a chapel and became the parish church. Previously it had been the mother church of Mackworth. It has a fine 12th-century doorway. When the church was rebuilt in 1866–67, a south aisle was added and the doorway had to be rebuilt, and some of the sandstone blocks were put back in the wrong position. The yew tree in the churchyard is over 1,000 years old and is said to be heard whispering and groaning to itself, especially in late autumn, when the dark wet nights are drawing in – protestation, perhaps, at the cold weather. They say that if you place your ear very close to the trunk of the tree you can hear a heartbeat! To the rear of the church and near to the wrought-iron fencing is a lamp-post. It is here that the ghostly figure of a monk has been seen walking in haste towards the church, only to vanish through the stonework of the building as if another building or doorway once existed there. He is dressed in a black habit, his face ashen, lips colourless and tightly fixed. One local who encountered the ghost described him as being 'determined looking with stern eyes' but not having an 'unkind face'.

No one seems to know who the monk is and there is no recorded evidence about anything tragic ever having happened on the site. Local children will not venture there after dark, although some dare each other to do so, for fear of meeting him.

Barrow on Trent church door. The phantom figure of a young man haunts this enigmatic doorway.

Barrow on Trent Church

The ghost of artist George Turner, as well as a boy tragically killed by a bull, is said to haunt St Wilfred's Church in Barrow on Trent. Barrow is a quiet, unspoilt Derbyshire village, sited between the River Trent and the Trent and Mersey Canal, about five miles south of Derby.

The old Manor House and grounds, together with fishing rights in the Trent, were given to the Methodist Ministers' Retirement Fund by the last owners, Mr and Mrs Houst, and in 1949 Manor Court was built, which comprised flats for retiring ministers who needed a home.

An old farmhouse called the Walnuts was where the family of artist George Turner lived in the 19th century. Many of his landscapes were painted in this area.

St Wilfred's Church is a Grade I listed building. It dates from about the 13th century, possibly on the site of an older church mentioned in the Domesday Book. Its Norman arcade still has its original, if much restored, columns. The base of the square tower and the north aisle are 14th century, while the upper part of the tower is from the 15th century. It contains an alabaster effigy of a priest from the 14th century.

The churchyard is said to be haunted by the famous painter, George Turner, who has been seen with brush and easel seated as if painting the church. His ghost is usually spotted on warm summer evenings.

Another frequent ghost is that of a young man who is seen coming through an old door. One local woman claims to

Barrow on Trent church. The ghost of the famous artist George Turner haunts St Wilfred's Church.

have seen him on a regular basis: 'I often wave to him and he likewise always waves back,' she said. He is described as quite small in stature and wearing simple breeches and shirt.

Haunted Christ Painting

No one knows for sure the origin of this unusual oil-on-wood painting, with a gilded carved frame in the form of a crown of thorns, but it is thought to date from the latter part of the 19th century and is believed to be French.

Haunted religious statues and paintings are not that unusual. There have been hundreds of accounts of statues that cry tears of blood. Other cultures have also reported strange incidents to do with religious icons.

The owner of the painting, July McGoverin of Mickleover, recounts the strange tale of the haunted painting in her own words.

'As a child, I remember the painting hanging in my father's library. I was one of four children and none of us would go into that room for fear of seeing the face in the painting change. Sometimes it would be frowning and sometimes it would be laughing. The face often appeared to be more forward in the painting and yet at other times it appeared to be further back. The colours of the painting also changed;

at times it would seem to be vibrant, the red of the blood bright crimson, almost real.

'When I was around eight years old, I remember my mother letting out a terrible scream. We all rushed to see what the matter was and we found her in the library, staring at the picture. At that time my grandmother was very ill, she lived in Canada, and my mother had been very worried about her. She claimed that the picture had spoken to her and had said

The haunted Christ. This atmospheric and haunting oil painting cries blood-red tears at Easter and emanates a curious perfume.

that my grandmother was now at peace. Shortly after that, we received news that my grandmother had passed away.

'On another occasion, we all awoke to a strange smell in the house. The smell was so strong that we all wondered where it was coming from; we soon found out that the smell, not dissimilar to violets, was coming from the room with the picture in. This smell was to continue on and off to the present day.

'My parents weren't overly religious and neither I, nor my brother and sisters, ever went to church. At one point my mother became so concerned that she called in a priest to have the picture and the house blessed. The priest went into the room and shortly afterwards returned ashen white, and told my mother and father to burn the picture immediately. He wouldn't say why, just that it should be burnt.

'On another occasion, my brother Kenny called me into his room and said that he was worried because he had things on his mind and, while in the library, the picture had spoken to him, telling him that everything would be ok. This hadn't bothered him, and he was contemplating telling my father what had happened. He never did, but from that day onward he refused to ever enter that room again.

'My other two sisters also refused to go into that room, ever since they had witnessed the picture crying a blood-red tear one Easter when they had been in the room. The picture always seemed to cry when some world disaster was about to take place, or at religious points of the year like Easter and Christmas.

'Time passed and I eventually left home for university. I didn't give the picture much thought after that. I met and married a wonderful man, developed my career, had children, and life continued in a fairly normal way. I would regularly visit my parents, but I would still not go into the library.

'After my father died, I went to stay with my mother for a few weeks to help out. I was cleaning one day when I realised that I would have to clean in the library. Eventually I plucked up enough courage and decided that I would go into the room but avert my gaze from the picture; I noticed as soon as I entered the room that the picture had gone! I never bothered to ask my mother where it had vanished to.

'A few years later my mother passed away, and my brother and I were given the task of sorting out her estate. We packed everything away and dispensed many of her personal items to friends and family according to her will. Then we had the job of sorting out the attic, which was crammed with junk. Halfway through the chore, my brother let out a gasp – he had found the haunted picture. I laughed at him and dismissed any childhood fear that I once had about the picture, took it from him, immediately went downstairs and deposited it on the skip with all the other rubbish and thought nothing more of it.

'Later that night, about 3am, I woke up from a troubled sleep; someone had been calling my name. I was wide awake and knew what I had to do; the urge to get out of bed and reclaim the picture was overwhelming. At that time I lived about 40 miles from my mother's house but that didn't deter me, nor did the torrential rain that was beating down. I drove to my mother's house (I didn't even tell my husband that I was going, I left him sleeping), got the picture, put it into the boot of my car and drove home again, soaking wet.

'Eventually, I fished it out of the car and was brave enough to hang it in the dining room. This was a mistake, as my children soon began to complain that the picture was staring at them as well as exuding a peculiar smell. My youngest child became hysterical when he claimed that the picture had spoken to him and when we examined the picture it had a red substance flowing down its face.

'I took down the picture and deposited it in the attic, where it has remained. Every so often, strange noises come from the attic and the house is pervaded with strange smells, but I have learned to live with it.'

The Derbyshire Royal Infirmary

The majority of hospitals across Derbyshire and, indeed, all over England, are said to be haunted by spirits not at rest. Due to the very nature of their establishments, tending to those who are very sick and dying, it is unsurprising to find that many who work in such buildings state that they believe many souls of those who passed away under such tragic circumstances remain to haunt the place of their death.

The Derbyshire Royal Infirmary is said to be the haunt of many such spirits. Two of these, which have been seen most frequently, are that of a grey lady who wanders the hallways and wards, checking the patients, and the apparition of a doctor who, it is believed, met his death by falling down a lift shaft on the western side of the building.

The first ghost has been given the nicknames 'the Lady with the Lamp' and 'Florrie', as she is believed to be the apparition of Florence Nightingale, who was famously associated with Derbyshire.

Florence Nightingale was the second child of Edward William Shaw, who later changed his name to Nightingale. He named Florence after the beautiful city in Italy in which she was born. Her father

Florence Nightingale, 'the Lady with the Lamp' is said to wander the older parts of the Derbyshire Royal Infirmary. Florence has appeared leaning over patients before vanishing into thin air.

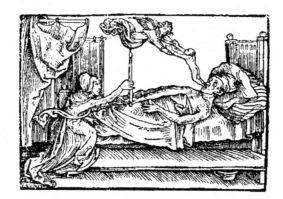

The Angel of Death taking the soul.

inherited a great deal of property, among which was Lea Hurst, a charming 17th-century gabled farmhouse in Derbyshire. Later, Edward also built Willersley Castle, which overlooks the River Derwent, near Matlock Bath.

Florence's international fame came during the Crimean War. So disturbed was she by the horrors of war that she could barely tear herself away from the sick and the dying, tending to as many as she could. Her patients therefore named her 'the Lady with the Lamp'.

In 1856, Florence returned to Derbyshire to her home at Lea Hurst, quietly avoiding the locals who wished to pay homage to a woman who had done so much for the wounded soldiers.

During the next 50 years, Florence was to change the face of nursing, consistently petitioning the Government for medical changes throughout the country. She died on 13 August 1910.

Florence's ghost is also said to haunt her beloved home, Lea Hurst, which was presented to the Royal Surgical Aid Society in 1951. Her apparition has been seen wandering along a top corridor and descending the stairs.

When her ghost has been witnessed by members of staff at the Derbyshire Royal Infirmary, she is said to be seen inspecting the patients, and, like her nickname, is always carrying a lamp. When staff have approached the phantom, in the belief that it is another member of staff, she simply vanishes before their eyes.

Ticknall lock-up. Strange noises are heard emanating from this ancient prison cell.

Ticknall Church

The Church of St George was built on the site of the former Church of Thomas Beckett in 1831, by Stevens, as good honest simple Gothic Revival. It has a west tower with the recessed spire usual in the Perpendicular style of this part of the country. The aisle arcades have octagonal piers.

The old church had become too small for the growing population of 1,281 residents, compared with approximately 750 now. When they tried to demolish the old church, parts proved resistant to gunpowder and picturesque remains are still standing, namely the west wall and the altar window.

The figure of a blue lady has been seen kneeling by the altar window as if she is in deep prayer, her eyes raised to the heavens. She is said to look saintly in appearance. Other spirits not at rest in the graveyard

Ticknall Church arch. The praying figure of a 'Blue Lady' appears as if she is in deep prayer. Other ghosts not at rest include a 'golden-haired boy' dressed in Elizabethan attire.

are a small golden-haired boy who seems to be lost, dressed in Elizabethan-style clothing; he stands near to the church with his head in his hands, sobbing. When approached he vanishes into thin air, with his sobs being the last thing heard.

Chellaston School. The former Headmaster's House, which was demolished towards the turn of the new millennium. The building was said to be the haunt of the headmaster and his wife. The smell of fried bacon was often noticed in the early morning when staff arrived for work.

Chellaston Infant School

At the end of School Lane in Chellaston stands Chellaston Infant School, one of the largest infant schools in the suburbs of Derby. The school first opened in 1878 and became an infant school in 1967, following the timely, and indeed needful, opening of Chellaston Junior School.

The school has undertaken several renovations over the last hundred years. The headmaster's house, a charming cottage-style building, part of the original late-19th-century school, was once situated central to the other school buildings before being demolished towards the turn of the new millennium.

The house was reputed to be haunted; many strange supernatural occurrences took place here. One such event, witnessed by two members of staff, concerns the stock room – a tiny box-room situated upstairs at the rear of the house. Prior to the demolition of the building, the aforesaid members of staff were emptying the rooms, moving stock out of the house and into other areas of the school.

The two ladies were carrying pots of poster paint when one was accidentally dropped, crashing to the floor, the contents spilling over the carpet. In her annoyance, the lady swore aloud and immediately after doing so, the lights in the building dimmed, casting murky shadows around them. The two staff members joked together, stating that the headmaster and his wife obviously did not approve of such disrespectful language spoken in their home. In response, the lady in question apologised aloud. To her surprise, the brightness of the lights immediately returned and normality was restored.

While the contents of the building were continued to be emptied, school staff often noted the distinct smell of fried bacon, particularly in the early morning, as members were seated downstairs in the Staff Room. Although no ghostly figures were actually seen, some members of staff believed that the headmaster and his wife were trying to communicate with them and the mouth-watering smell of bacon was perhaps the couple's way of trying to entice them into leaving the building intact. Alas, this failed, and the building was demolished, despite the unearthly attempts of the dead!

Derby Cathedral

The rapid increase in the population of England in the late 19th and early 20th century resulted in the creation of new bishoprics and several hitherto 'ordinary' churches becoming cathedrals. There was neither the time nor the money to build the sort of grand new cathedrals which had risen in Norman times, and new bishops were designated existing churches as their seats. Thus, in 1927, All Saints' Church in Derby became Derby Cathedral.

Thought to have been founded by King Edmund in AD943, All Saints' has been altered considerably over the centuries. At the beginning of the 18th century, the only thing that could have been said to have been striking about this church was its tower, 212ft tall – the second highest parish church tower in England – and built in the time of Henry VIII.

In 1723 the church was deemed unsafe and it seems that no one was prepared to do anything about it until a particularly courageous churchman, the Revd Dr Michael Hutchinson, ordered that the entire structure – except the tower – should be demolished.

The decision was unpopular with local people but shortly afterwards plans for the rebuilding were submitted by James Gibbs, who became famous for many of his churches, including St Mary-le-Strand, and perhaps his most famous work, St Martin-in-the Fields, in London. The designs for a new All Saints' were accepted and

Derby Cathedral. Numerous ghosts haunt this site including a 'White Lady', former unhappy executioner John Crossland and the enigmatic Bonnie Prince Charlie.

work soon began, resulting in the magnificent church which we know today as Derby Cathedral.

Working in association with Gibbs was Robert Bakewell, an ironsmith whose striking wrought-iron screen remains one of the most notable features of the cathedral's interior. Other notable features include the remarkable baldachin and several memorial carvings, many to notable Derbyshire families. One of these is Bess of Hardwick's monument, which was built and completed within her own lifetime.

Another interesting memorial is a tablet on the south wall near the steps to St Katherine's Chapel, which commemorates an historic visit from Prince Charles Edward Stuart, who visited All Saints' in December 1745. The Young Pretender had marched with his army, virtually unchallenged, from Carlisle. On reaching Derby his troops were stationed about the town and the prince is said to have ordered the bells of All Saints' to be rung and, with his officers accompanying him, he attended a service at the church.

Several ghosts are said to haunt the vicinity of Derby Cathedral, including that of Charles Edward Stuart, seen by a lady who lived in a building, now a shop, across the road. She told me her story of how she often sees a man in Jacobite dress walk into the cathedral: 'On many occasions I had seen the vague ghostly shape of a man in Jacobite costume walking near the cathedral. Being familiar with the story of Bonnie Prince Charlie and his visit to Derby I presumed that it was the prince retracing his footsteps, perhaps trying to understand how it had all gone wrong for him. My mother once saw this figure and she too was convinced that it was the ghost of Bonnie Prince Charlie.'

It is interesting to note that a ghostly figure in Cavalier-style dress has also been spotted not too far from this spot at the Silk Mill public house.

Many other ghosts have been seen about Derby Cathedral, including a 'white lady' seen walking down the steps at the back of the church, a young woman seen crying and a small boy.

Also said to wander the grounds is the unhappy ghost of John Crossland, a former executioner and originally himself a criminal, who was granted a pardon on the understanding that he would become the executioner for the sentence of death passed on his father and brother. This he agreed to do and from then on he became the

Saint Mary's, Bridge Gate. St Mary's can be seen here in the background with St Mary's Bridge in the foreground, the haunt of three executed priests. To the foreground, left, may be seen the former Saint Alkmund's Church, an ancient place of pilgrimage which was said to hold the bones of Saint Alkmund himself. His sarcophagus is said to have miraculous healing powers.

busiest executioner in the county, frequently being used by several other shires. His ghost is said to be seen wandering the grounds at the side of the cathedral, seeking to find peace for his tormented and guilty soul.

Saint Mary's Church, Bridge Gate

St Mary's Church was built by Augustus Pugin, who also drew designs for the Houses of Parliament. Before 1840, Catholics in Derby were allowed to worship only in the Catholic Chapel in Chapel Street, but, with the large influx of Irish immigrants to Derby with the building of the railways, land was purchased on Bridge Gate for a new Catholic church. It was, incidentally, Pugin's first Catholic church, and although he designed over 100 churches altogether, St Mary's has always been considered his masterpiece.

The ghost of a priest has been seen on the right-hand side of St Mary's Church. The story goes that a newly-installed priest was coming down the stairs with three other priests. Arriving in the main church the new priest mentioned to the others that he had not realised that there would be four other priests there that day. The others looked confused and told him that he must be mistaken as they were only three and he now made four. The new priest looked shocked and told the others that they had not long been seated upstairs for their meeting when an older priest with grey hair had joined them.

Little Chester

There is much evidence to suggest that as early as AD80, a Roman fort existed beside the River Derwent, at Little Chester, which the Romans called Derventio. Archaeological excavations of the site revealed that the defences of the fort were rectangular in shape, enclosing an estimated area of seven acres, being surrounded by two deep ditches placed 100ft apart. A clay rampart was later added, and later still the site was reinforced with a thick stone wall some 10ft to 15ft high.

The playing field and car park at the junction of City Road and old Chester

Road is probably where the main headquarters building stood. It is also thought that several other buildings occupied the site, including an infirmary, an armoury and other smaller units, making the whole site of Little Chester self-sufficient.

Although no inscriptions have yet been found at Little Chester, there are references from other ancient sources where the later name Derbentione appears between Lutudarum and Salinac in a seventh-century town listing (the Ravenna Cosmography). The only indication of how many soldiers were

stationed on the site lies in the size of the fort, which covered seven acres and therefore must have housed one of the bigger auxiliary forts. The largest cavalry unit (alla milliaria), meaning a thousand horsemen, was believed to be stationed in Britain, at Stanwix, on Hadrian's Wall. The unit appearing to be most suitably placed at Little Chester would have been a cohors equitata milliaria, which consisted of 10 centuries of infantry and, in total, five of these units were stationed in Britain.

Much of the site at Little Chester has been excavated, although there is almost certainly a great deal yet to be uncovered. Some interesting finds, however, have surfaced at the site, among which is a grindstone block – crudely carved in the shape of a shrine containing within it the nude figure of a horned man. This was found in the last century by a gardener digging near the River Derwent. This grindstone block, known as the Mercury Stone, has so far been the only carving found at the site, and, although originally the figure was thought to represent the Roman god Mercury, it is now believed to be the horned god of the Brigantes – whose cult became combined with that of the Roman deity. The Mercury Stone is at present on display at Derby Museum and Art Gallery. The carved stone figure is also believed by many to represent a horned god of fertility, worshipped by ancient Pagans and still held sacred by modern-day witches.

In November 1978, a burial ground was discovered when trees and undergrowth were being removed by bulldozers on the Racecourse Playing Fields. This ancient graveyard is believed to have existed on the east side of the encampment as Roman law stated that no burials, except those of young children, were allowed within the town. Other burial grounds were also uncovered on the Racecourse. One particular grave site, containing both inhumations and cremations, had unusual features: several of the interments had been mutilated prior to or while being buried: the left hand of one had been severed, others had been decapitated and, in several cases, the heads had been placed between the knees and two others had been buried face down.

The reason for these strange rites at the time of burial perhaps dates back to an old superstitious belief concerning witches and dark sorcery. When a dead person was believed to have been a witch or black magician, or in any way connected with magic and witchcraft, it was the custom to bury them face down or remove their head in order that they should not rise from the grave and haunt the living.

Another grave site, not far from where the mutilated remains were found, consisted of three male bodies, one of which was found to have two coins placed upon him. These coins were probably placed there in the belief that they would be accepted by the deity Charon, whose job it was to ferry the souls of the dead across the dark waters of the River Styx on their journey to the Underworld.

Many buildings at Chester Green, especially those buildings close to the remains of the excavated Roman encampment, are known to be haunted. One interesting story comes from a lady who lives in a house there, which probably dates back to a time when part of the building was used for storage by the Romans. Although the ghost has not made a personal appearance, he, or she, has manifested themselves in other ways. The ghost frequently clears away household rubbish, closes opened curtains in the living room, and has been known on several occasions to wash dirty crockery, much to the appreciation of the owner.

Another instance, seemingly more frightening, is the appearance of a spectre which is said to resemble a Roman centurion. One Derby man claims to have seen this figure one dark, foggy winter's evening while walking home from work. 'The ghost,' I was informed, 'just glared at me with very large eyes.' This gentleman went on to state that he had not waited about to question the apparition, but had hurried home to the waiting comfort of his front room and a stiff drink.

A round house, located at Derventio at the old Derby Racecourse site. One lady claims to have entered into a 'slip in time' when she came upon a scene from the ancient past, with stalls, people and the smells and sounds of market traders.

Chester Green. Whole regiments of Roman soldiers are seen marching across the area. Many of the houses around Chester Green are said to be haunted. Archaeology digs have revealed several Roman cemeteries.

Many times over the last decade I have received requests from people living in the Chester Green area, who have asked me to investigate a haunting that they feel they might have. Several of these people had indeed disturbed forces within their homes, while others were perhaps suffering from over-active imaginations.

Other ghosts have been seen in the area, including a whole regiment of Roman soldiers seen and heard marching one night near the River Derwent. The apparition of a ghostly child with snow-white hair has been observed near the site of a Roman well. One lady who has lived in the area for many years claims that the area of Little Chester has always had the reputation of being haunted by sinister things. This lady also claims that since excavations were carried out in the area in 1978, even more ghosts have been seen. She further stated that the excavations had disturbed spirits which would have been best left untroubled, in what should have been their final resting places.

The Headless Cross, Friar Gate

Derby suffered several times from the plague, perhaps being worst affected in 1592 when 464 people perished. Local farmers refused to trade with the townspeople and it is said that grass grew in the Market Place from lack of people and business. As the plague continued, it was feared that there would be a famine until, at last, farmers in the surrounding countryside agreed to trade with the people of the town under the condition that money for the payment of provisions was left in bowls of vinegar at the Headless Cross on Nun's Green. The farmers returned later to collect their money.

The 'Hedles Cros', or 'Broken Crosse', as it has been recorded, is thought to date from the 14th century and by the 15th it had been recorded as already having lost its top. At one time the cross was moved to the Derby Arboretum where it stood for many years, having a reputation even then of being haunted. Eventually the Headless Cross was moved back to the top of Friar Gate, probably quite close to where it originally stood.

Two ghosts have been seen near the Headless Cross, one of which is said to be that of a dog sitting. The other is alleged to be the figure of a lady in grey – although she is sometimes in white – 'coming out of the stone'. Some claim that the ghost of another lady which is often seen in the Arboretum is in some way connected with the cross, while others believe that the same ghost now haunts both Friar Gate and the Arboretum.

The Vengeful Dead

Is there any wonder that Derby is the Ghost Capital of England when we consider its dark and violent past? Like many cities, Derby has had its fair share

Friar Gate. The Headless Cross was moved back to its original place from the Arboretum Park. A ghostly dog as well as mysterious balls of light haunt this ancient carved rock.

Derby Arboretum. The figure of a lady in grey haunts Derby Arboretum and the Headless Cross. Many believe that the grey lady that haunts the cross and the park are one and the same.

of executions. One particular gruesome form of death under law was as follows:

'That you be taken back to the prison whence you came to a low dungeon, into which no light can enter; that you be laid on your back on the bare floor with a cloth around your loins but elsewhere naked; that there be set upon your body a weight of iron as great as you can bear and greater; that you have no sustenance except on the first day a morsel

of coarse bread and on the second day three draughts of stagnant water from the pool nearest the prison door and on the third another morsel of coarse bread as before. If after three days you are still alive, the weight will be taken from your body and a large sharp stone placed beneath your back and the weight replaced.'

A deaf mute woman was thus sentenced in the Shire Hall, St Mary's Gate, and pressed to death in 1665.

Accused persons who remained in the witness box in court were given three chances to plead guilty or not guilty. After the third time of asking, followed by time for reconsideration, 'judgement of penance' was passed – the above blood-curdling sentence.

This was the last time in England that this horrible execution was carried out and the woman's ghost is said still to wander in the cells which are preserved underneath Derby's Shire Hall, possibly the most ominous building remaining in Derby to this day. It was built in 1659 and was the scene of all the famous murder trials in Derbyshire. The Pentrich Martyrs were sentenced to be hanged, drawn and quartered there in 1817. That was the last time such a sentence was passed in England.

The following list is a sample of some more barbaric executions that took place here.

I August 1556

Joan Waste was burnt as a heretic in Windmill Pit, on the Burton Road, in Derby. She was a blind woman who, during the reign of Edward VI, had attended the services of the church. After Queen Mary came to the throne, she was accused before the Bishop of the Diocese of maintaining that the sacrament was only a memorial or representation of the body of Christ, and the elements were mere bread and wine.

This opinion she was required to renounce, but after persisting in it she received sentence of condemnation. After a sermon in the church, she was led to the stake just off Burton Road and there burned, holding Roger Waste, her brother, by the hand, praying and desiring those around her to pray.

1608

Five men and a woman were executed at Tapton Bridge, Chesterfield, the Assizes having been held at Chesterfield owing to the prevalence of the plague at Derby.

25 July 1683

Three Roman Catholic priests, Nicholas Garlick, Robert Ludlam and Richard Sympson, suffered martyrdom at Derby, being hanged, drawn and quartered.

1693

A farm girl in Swanwick was burned for murdering her master. This was the last case of death by burning at the stake in Derbyshire.

23 March 1732

John Hewitt and Rosamund Clerenshaw were executed for poisoning Hannah Hewitt in Derby. They were executed in their shrouds.

2 March 1738

Richard Woodward was hanged in Derby for highway robbery.

1757

Thomas Hulley was hanged for returning from transportation.

1 April 1785

William and George Grooby and James Peat were hanged for burglary in Derby.

'It is now more than sixty years,' said the *Derby Mercury*, 'since there were so many executed at one time upon our gallows; the persons who suffered then were named Rock, Lyon, and Shaw, and we believe their crime was counterfeiting the current coin of the realm. Peat wrote on the prison doors with chalk: "Calm and Composed, my soul a journey takes; No guilt that troubles, nor a heart that akes."'

29 March 1788

Thomas Grundy was hanged for murdering his brother. After the execution, his body was publicly dissected in the presence of a great number of spectators.

10 April 1795

Thomas Neville was hanged for burglary.

He was carried to execution in a mourning coach, attended by a hearse, where he assisted his executioner to fasten the rope to the tree, after which he drew his cap over his face and leapt from the cart into eternity.

19 March 1803

William Wells was hanged for murder in Barlborough.

About a minute after he had been hanged the rope slipped and he fell to the ground; the executioner was therefore under the necessity of tying him up a second time. His body was given to the surgeons for dissection.

9 April 1813

Paul Mason, Richard Hibbert and Peter Henshaw were hanged for burglary.

They were executed on the new drop, in front of the County Gaol, before an immense crowd of spectators.

8 March 1815

Anthony Lingard was hanged for murder.

This was the last case of gibbetting in the county of Derby. The body was afterwards removed to Wardlow Miers, and hung in chains near to the house where the crime was perpetrated.

Lingard's brother William was, 11 years later, sentenced at Derby Assizes for highway robbery and assault, and was reprieved. William Lingard committed the robbery within view of the gibbett on which the bleaching bones of his brother were hanging.

15 August 1817

John Brown, Thomas Jackson, George Booth and John King were hanged for arson in North Wingfield.

In describing the execution, the *Derby Mercury* of that date says: 'As every fact which may tend to illustrate the principles of human action deserves notice, it is worth observing that a heavy shower happening while the doomed men were singing the hymn, two of them deliberately retreated to the shelter of an umbrella which was expanded on the drop, and a third placed himself under cover of the doorway. The inconvenience of being wet was felt and avoided by men who knew they had not five minutes longer to live!'

7 November 1817

Brandreth, Ludlam and Turner, the 'Pentrich Plotters', were executed in Derby. It was the last instance of the old penalty of high treason, hanging, drawing and quartering.

Cavalry stood on guard during the execution. It was the prisoners were first dragged round the prison yard on hurdles, were then hanged for half an hour, and their bodies afterwards were cut down.

The executioner then struck the heads

off the bodies and, seizing the head of Brandreth by the hair, showed the ghastly countenance to the multitude, exclaiming: 'Behold the head of the traitor, Jeremiah Brandreth.'

The crowd, 'as if under the impulse of a sudden frenzy,' separated in all directions, but equanimity was restored,

'and the separation and exhibition of the remaining heads was witnessed with the greatest order and decorum'.

The executioners were masked and their names were kept a profound secret. The poet Shelley witnessed the scene.

The block is still to be seen in Derby Prison, where its wood hangs damp; always damp – so it has been averred – it has given rise to the tradition that the block of the unhappy men has not dried and never will.

22 March 1819

Hannah Docking (aged 16) was hanged for poisoning another little girl.

1 April 1847

John Platts was hanged for murder in Chesterfield.

This was a public execution in front of the County Gaol and was witnessed by 20,000 people.

11 April 1862

Richard Thorley was hanged for the murder of Eliza Morrow.

This was the last public execution in Derby.

21 November 1881

Alfred Gough was hanged for the murder of Eleanor Windley, aged six, in Brimington.

10 August 1888

Arthur Thomas Delaney was hanged for the murder of his wife in Chesterfield.

30 July 1902

John Bedford was hanged for the murder of Nancy Price in Duckmanton.

29 December 1905

John Silk was hanged for the murder of his mother in Chesterfield.

Theatrical Spirits

Most theatres across Britain are reported to have at least one ghost roaming their corridors; some are said to be the apparitions of famous actors and actresses who once performed there. For example, the ghost of the 19th-century actress Sarah Bernhardt is said to walk the corridors of the Theatre Royal in Brighton, pushing past people before walking through a wall to where, it is said, her dressing room once stood. Sarah Siddons, one of Britain's leading actresses of the 19th century, is reputed to haunt Bristol's Old Vic theatre.

Derby has its own fair share of ghostly tales connected with its theatres, past and present.

Derby Playhouse

Derby Playhouse opened in the Eagle Centre in 1975. It is believed that the theatre has more than one ghost; reports by previous workers state that the ghost of a woman has been seen in the ladies' toilets and members of the public have experienced blasts of cold air and the feeling that they are 'being watched', especially if they have visited the toilets alone when they have been empty.

Jennifer, who acted on stage at the Playhouse some years ago as a teenager, recalls the following:

'One night during production week we were having our technical rehearsal in preparation for the opening night. The rehearsal was taking some time and we were working quite late into the evening. Everyone was tired and during some parts of the rehearsal process, when certain actors were not required on stage, we would sit in the auditorium and watch the process. My friend Emma and I were watching the rehearsal progress from the back row of the seating area but had lost interest and were both tired after such a long day. We decided to stretch our legs and go for a short walk to try and wake ourselves up, so we made our way to the double doors at the back of the auditorium which led to the bar area. As I opened the door, and looking out to the bar area, I saw a figure of a man dressed in a black suit moving quickly before disappearing behind the bar. At first I thought it was a member of the bar staff and was puzzled that the bar was open at such a late hour when the theatre was presently closed to members of the public. I didn't think much of it, but Emma was obviously confused too as she commented to me on our way to the toilets, "I didn't know they'd kept the bar open". We stopped halfway in our walk and decided to go back and investigate. There was nobody to be seen in or around the bar area; the shutters of the bar were down and the door was locked. At the time we didn't think that what we had experienced was anything other-worldly, but on further enquiry we discovered that a ghost of a man fitting the same description had been seen on more than one occasion around the bar area and restaurant.'

One of the dressing rooms of Derby Playhouse is also said to be haunted, although members of staff do not tell actors which dressing room it is, perhaps for fear that they will refuse to perform at the theatre!

The Grand Theatre

The Grand Theatre on Babington Lane in Derby, which was designed by Andrew Melville, opened on 25 March 1886 but burned down within a month of opening. During that fateful night, Melville was sitting in the auditorium awaiting the commencement of what he hoped to be a successful show (Edward Terry and his comedy company), when noises were heard coming from backstage. On investigation, Melville discovered that one of the borders was on fire, a fire which quickly spread to surrounding scenery and parts of the stage. The fire brigade were alerted and actors and members of the audience were asked to leave as quickly as possible. However, one of the actors, John Adams, was discovered unconscious and despite being taken as quickly as possible to the Infirmary in a butcher's cart, passed away during the journey. The badly burnt corpse of a carpenter, James Locksley, was also later discovered by the stage door; he had been unable to escape the fire.

Andrew Melville promised to rebuild his theatre, despite the large renovation costs, and within six months of the fire, on 13 November, Derby's Grand Theatre re-opened.

The world premiere of the first stage adaptation of *Dracula* was staged at the theatre in 1924 and the building remains to this day the site of many spooky happenings. Since the days when the site housed a theatre, the building has had many incarnations, mainly being home to nightclubs of various guises over the last decade.

The ghostly tales continue to be told; past workers state that some of their colleagues refused to go into certain parts of the building unless accompanied by another, and figures have been seen in the upper storeys. Perhaps these sightings are the ghosts of John Adams or James Locksley, who tragically lost their lives all those years ago. Incidentally, it is said that Gower Street, the road opposite the building, was once known as 'Blood Lane'.

The Derby Hippodrome

Just a few yards away from the Grand Theatre, on the corner of Green Lane and Macklin Street, lies the Derby Hippodrome, which opened in 1914 as a 2,300-capacity variety house offering Music Hall-style entertainment. Stars of international fame such as Gracie Fields, George Formby, Max Miller and Flanagan and Allen all performed here. It is said that Bud Flanagan composed *Underneath the Arches* during one of his visits to Derby, while sheltering from the rain under the railway bridge in Ford Street.

The theatre was built on the site of Derby's first private lunatic asylum, which was closed shortly after a shocking incident where one of the inmates cut a warder's

throat. The ghostly apparition of this warder has been seen in the building; he appears to be covered in blood and is seen staggering and clutching at his throat.

The Guildhall Theatre

The theatre is host to many productions from various travelling theatre companies and amateur dramatic groups. One lady, Cath, who was a member of one such amateur dramatic company, discussed a strange occurrence she experienced during a performance at the theatre.

'During the opening night of a show I was in at the Guildhall, I had a particularly quick change of costume in between scenes. I took my costume to the toilets with me and was hastily changing, when I heard the sound of someone humming a tune in the cubicle next to me. I was startled because I had not heard anyone enter the room. Thinking it was my fellow actress, I called out her name and was about to ask her why she wasn't on stage. However, the humming abruptly stopped. I called out her name again, but there was still no reply. Having got changed, I opened the door and stepped out into the room. The cubicle next to me was empty and there was nobody in the room. I was frightened and immediately left, hurrying to the wings at the side of the stage where, to my astonishment, I discovered everybody was on stage. For the rest of the performances, I remained at the side of the stage when I was not required to perform, taking comfort from the sound and sight of my fellow actors. Prior to this strange experience I had refused to believe in ghosts or anything supernatural, considering all such related stories to be rubbish and made up. However, having gone over the events of that night several times in my head, I cannot come to any logical explanation for what I experienced. Suffice to say, I have never returned to the theatre to perform there!'

Beneath the Guildhall is a labyrinth of tunnels and catacombs. One of the tunnels used to link the old police lock-up in Lock-Up Yard to the Assize Courts, which were at that time in the Guildhall. Many prisoners trudged along these tunnels from the lock-up to the courts where they were sentenced and were often then taken away to be executed. Many people have reported hearing ghostly footsteps along these tunnels. Also, the ghost of a little boy has been seen, dressed in rags. Workers in the tunnels have chased after him, shouting, and although thorough searches have been made, no sign of the boy has been found.

Derby Assembly Rooms

As in other towns, the Assembly Rooms in Derby was a popular meeting place in the 18th century, where young people danced and the elderly people played cards while keeping a watchful eye on their offspring. The aim of an assembly was to bring all sorts and classes of people together harmoniously, but in Derby this was not to be. By 1714 there had evolved two very separate assemblies: one at the corner of the Market Place and Full Street for the gentry of the county, and one for the lesser mortals of the town. This second assembly was situated at Moote Hall or meeting place, part of which still exists, although it is now incorporated into the modern façade of Nando's Restaurant on the corner of the Market Place and Iron Gate.

A bizarre incident happened there on the night of 5 December 1745. People had come from far and wide to a reception held for Prince Charles Edward Stuart, who had arrived in Derby on his way to take the English crown. The crush of people was so great that a table bearing the Royal Standard was overturned and the standard was broken. This was considered a bad omen by many of the prince's army and, although the decision was taken on military grounds alone, following that fateful reception the order was given for the retreat of the Highland army back north. There eventually followed, of course, the Battle of Culloden, the slaughter and transportation of hundreds of Scots, the burning of their homes, the killing of their cattle and, eventually, the Highland Clearances.

A county assembly had been built in Derby in 1714, and an even larger building was erected on the Market Place in 1763. This was badly damaged by fire 200 years later and a much larger Assembly Rooms, opened in 1977, now occupies the old site on the Market Place, including the site of the Duke of Newcastle's house, where King Charles I stayed in 1637. The modern Assembly Rooms complex still provides entertainment for Derbyshire people as well as playing host to national exhibitions and sporting events.

According to many people, the present building is haunted. Mick Taylor, the house manager, was in the building at 3am one morning, standing in the concourse with his back to the Darwin Suite. Also present was another member of staff. Mr Taylor turned around – why, he did not know – and saw an elderly lady dressed in

Victorian costume. She appeared to have no legs and seemed to be floating. He alerted his colleague, who also turned around, and both witnessed the figure gliding across the floor before disappearing.

On many other occasions, security guards have seen what appeared to be a ring of children dancing in the Darwin Suite and have often reported the eerie sounds of laughter when there is no one in the building.

The new Assembly Rooms were built between 1973 and 1977. As the footings and foundations were being installed a builder reported seeing what he and several work colleagues believed to be the remains of an old Viking ship – which is quite feasible as the site is close to the River Derwent. He reported the matter to his superiors but was told that because of a penalty clause in the contract, the work had to be finished on time and so hundreds of tons of concrete were poured over the remains of what might have proved to be one of Derby's most important links with the past.

Hours of the Living

Repton – Ghost Citadel of Mercia

Since ancient times, the village of Repton, in the lands of Mercia, has been a sacred place held in high spiritual esteem by wise and holy men alike. Is there something magical in the earth? Is there something special about this place? No one really knows for sure. Some people believe that it has a high psychic energy because ley-lines, like electrical power veins that run between historical and ancient, often Pagan monuments, criss-cross through the area on their way to such places as Stonehenge, Glastonbury and our very own Stonehenge of the North: Arbor Low in north Derbyshire.

The Curse of Samuel Marshall

In the churchyard of St Wystan's, Repton, just to the right of the south porch, lying against a stone wall, are several headstones. One slate memorial is dedicated to a Samuel Marshall, aged 21, who was murdered in 1786. His killer was caught but acquitted at trial for the lack of witnesses.

The inscription reads: 'To the memory of Samuel Marshall, who unfortunately fell a victim to a barbarous assassin on February 14th 1786, in the 21st year of his age.' It is followed by:

> By murd'rous hand my thread of life was broke,
> Dreadful the hour and terrible the stroke,
> Repent! Thou wicked spoiler of my youth,
> Behold me here! Consider parents both,
> See from thy bloody hand what woes arise,
> While calls for vengeance pierce the lofty skies,

St Wystan's Church, Repton. An ancient goblin that grants wishes – if caught – is said to live in the church tower.

Thou too must suffer, though thou escape the laws,
For God is just and will avenge my cause.

If you examine the headstone you will see it depicts a tree with five branches, one of which has been cut off with an axe representing the dead man, and the others representing his surviving brothers. A nearby gravestone is that of Samuel's grief-stricken father, who died in the following year.

Here is how the *Derby Mercury* reported the murder and subsequent trial at Derby Assizes:

'A most shocking murder was perpetrated on Saturday evening last on Samuel Marshall, a baker, of Repton.

'He was upon his return with an empty bread cart, having delivered his bread and cakes etc. at several villages and particularly at Rolleston (the next day being Wakes Sunday at that village). He had received cash, it is said, to the amount of six or seven pounds, and was making the best of his way home when his career was suddenly stopped by some villain or villains unknown.

'He was found about seven o'clock by one William Mountford, a labouring man, of Ticknall, who was passing by and saw the unhappy youth lying on the ground near the Navigation Bridge at Willington, and his body mangled in a frightful manner.

'He had received a violent blow on the head and also a deep cut behind the left ear, which seems to have been done with a penknife or some sharp instrument. They had cut his throat in such a manner that a piece of his flesh hung down to his chin, but had not penetrated his windpipe. His pockets were turned out, the contents taken.

'As soon as possible the neighbourhood was alarmed, the body removed to Repton, and a warrant, and a hue and cry issued by a worthy magistrate. Persons were despatched to search the most suspected places.

'Handbills were printed and dispersed (offering a reward of £40 over and above what is allowed by Act of Parliament), and every means used to bring the perpetrator of this inhuman deed to condign punishment. But, notwithstanding that several have been taken up on suspicion, yet after examination they have been discharged, nothing substantial appearing to incriminate them.'

A few days later the *Derby Mercury* reported, 'On Thursday night, about 10 o'clock, a young man named James Wheldon, of the village of Rolleston, near Burton upon Trent, was brought to the county gaol, charged on a violent suspicion of having committed the murder near Willington on the body of Samuel Marshall, baker.

'He, that day, underwent an examination of about eight hours before Sir Robert Bardett [Burdett?] Bart (one of His Majesty's Justices of the Peace). When a very minute enquiry was made, and that with the strictest impartiality and it appearing by many corroborating circumstances that the above young man might personally be suspected of perpetrating the horrid deed, he was committed for trial at the next Assizes.

'One particular we must not omit, which is that a blacksmith's hammer was found near the spot it was perpetrated in, having, it is supposed, been the instrument used on the barbarous occasion, and had been thrown over the hedge immediately after the murder.

'On the discovery of his hammer, several persons were despatched to Rolleston, and upon enquiry the blacksmith missed the hammer, and afterwards it came out on the oath of this man that he had lent the hammer to Wheldon several days prior to the murder. This circumstance the prisoner positively denies, saying he never borrowed a hammer from him in all his life. There are several other circumstances incriminating him but how far they may weigh in the views of a jury, time only can determine.'

The *Derby Mercury* reported on 23 March 1786, 'James Wheldon, charged with the murder of young Marshall, baker, of Repton, was acquitted after a hearing of nearly six hours.' Unfortunately there is no account of the trial itself.

In his 1971 article in the *Derbyshire Advertiser*, the late Mr H.J. Wain wrote, 'The story has been handed down that the prisoner was acquitted largely due to an alibi in his favour, sworn by a young woman he was about to marry, and also the refusal of the blacksmith to confirm his previous oath as to the identity of the hammer found near the scene of the crime. The young woman lived at Barrow-on-Trent and, on the evening of the trial, she set out to meet a friend returning from Derby with news of the result. On hearing that Wheldon had been acquitted, she "manifested the wildest fury, her shrieks and cries betokening the influence of insanity. At last, having uttered one of the most appalling maledictions that ever escaped human lips, she sank into a state of insensibility, which lasted for at least four hours".'

According to another account, the suspect was seen in after years to visit the spot where the crime was committed and also the churchyard, to gaze upon the gravestone of his victim. This account goes on to relate: 'Some time afterwards, Dr Chawner of Repton, an eminent practitioner, who had given evidence as a medical witness at Wheldon's trial and whose evidence bore strongly against him, was called upon at a late hour on a dark and tempestuous night by a stranger, who requested him to visit a patient whose name he had not before heard, and who resided at Measham, near Ashby-de-la-Zouch, and whose case was said to be one of extreme urgency.'

'The doctor got out his gig and, with the stranger as his guide, undertook the long journey. He arrived at the village in due course and was admitted into a house where, in a bed surrounded by drawn curtains, on the ground floor, lay his patient uttering loud and frequent groans. On pulling back the curtains, the doctor beheld to his amazement the distorted features of the accused assassin of Samuel Marshall. He feared at first he had been decoyed, and it was the intention of the sick man to exact revenge on him for giving evidence at his trial. But it was soon evident that Wheldon had no such intention, and indeed was alarmed by the appearance of the doctor who had been hastily summoned by a neighbour without Wheldon's knowledge.

'Dr Chawner, after various attempts to give relief to the sufferer, gazed at him for some time, while a series of awful sensations passed through his mind. The solemn hour of midnight, the raging storm with vivid flashes of lightning and deep bursts of thunder, the presence of a suspected murderer with what appeared to be a final and mortal struggle with a rapidly approaching end, impressed upon the mind of the contemplator a picture of the terrible destiny that awaits the evil-doer.'

So runs an imaginative account of the illness of James Wheldon some time after he had been acquitted of Marshall's murder. Unfortunately, it is not known when or where he died, or why a medical practitioner living in Repton should be called upon to attend an unknown patient residing in Measham. But the curse, written on the headstone of Samuel Marshall in the Repton churchyard by his grieving family, seems finally to have struck down his barbarous assassin, who, having managed to escape the hangman's noose, suffered a dreadful death.

The ghostly figure of a man, believed to be that of Marshall's killer, Wheldon, has been seen placing flowers at his victim's grave. His head is bowed, as if in grief, and he kneels to place the flowers before vanishing at the spot. Other reports

The grave of Samuel Marshall, Repton, murdered in 1786 aged 21. The perpetrator of Samuel's demise is still seen at the graveside; some say he seeks absolution for his terrible crime. Note the interesting grave carving, a tree with five branches, one of which has been cut off with an axe, representing the dead man and his surviving relatives.

say that it is Marshall himself, and his cries calling for vengeance still remain to 'pierce the lofty skies'.

The Haunting of St Wystan's Church

Repton village was at one time an extremely important religious centre. The first Christian church of converted English is thought to have been erected at Repton by four priests who travelled from Northumbria in the seventh century. The Church of St Wystan is believed to have been founded around the time of the Norman Conquest. Before that, the village is thought to have run not north to south, but east to west, along the banks of the River Trent rather than down the Repton Hartshorne Valley.

As a leading city of Mercia, Repton had an active history, which culminated in AD874 when the town and abbey were sacked by the Danes. Repton has long had an association with ghostly happenings and strange goings-on. At some time before the mid-19th century, the villagers were said to have gone out with lanterns to search for ghosts.

In 1861 three ghosts appeared at two in the morning and, crossing the churchyard, they mysteriously vanished. These ghosts were seen by a pupil of Repton School, which overlooks part of the churchyard. One writer a little later suggested that the three phantoms might well have vanished into a tunnel which, to this day, is still thought to exist somewhere in the churchyard. The tunnel, according to local legend, runs from the churchyard to Anchor Church, another very haunted place where eerie other-worldly creatures are said to dwell. A 17th-century grave-digger is also said to haunt the area around the church. At one time a village grave-digger reported being discomfited by the curious figure of a man who would stand watching him whenever he was digging a grave, from the shadow of some trees at the edge of the churchyard.

A far more sinister spirit, although not seen in recent times, is that of a demonic figure that appeared on numerous occasions bathed in wreathes of sulphurous smoke sitting on a gravestone. A similar supernatural creature has also been spotted in the crypt of St Wystan beneath the church. This remarkable crypt, which reputedly held the remains of the saint, is also the haunt of a hooded figure.

Perhaps the most famous ghost story at Repton is that of the Gallery Ghost, which is known to haunt Repton School. In 1853 Frederick Wickham-Railton, aged 14 years and eight months, was forced to run the gauntlet…a piece of foolery that many boys were forced to go through if their prefect deemed them to have committed an offence.

On the gallery, which the boys' bedrooms opened onto, Frederick was forced to run up and down three times while other boys lashed out at him with an assortment of wet towels and pillow cases. One boy, believed to have been Frederick's brother, tied an ink bottle into the end of his pillow case and, as Frederick passed, he lashed out at him, striking the boy violently on the head, killing him instantly.

Crypt Orb, St Wystan's Church, Repton. This unusual picture shows an orb which are said to be the disembodied souls caught on film. The crypt is haunted by a hooded figure. St Wystan's last remains are said to have rested here and the crypt is said to have peculiar healing powers.

From that day onwards the unhappy ghost of Frederick Wickham-Railton returned from the grave to haunt the winner of the annual steeplechase. His ghost has also been heard running up and down the gallery late at night.

Repton Church is also said to harbour the mischievous spirit of a goblin who is recorded as residing in the 14th-century spire and recessed tower. Only appearing at night – especially if there is a full moon – he will, if caught, grant mortals one wish, as long as the wish does not benefit the person who catches it, and the wish is made there and then.

The most peculiar ghost to haunt Repton churchyard is that of a tall male figure seen wandering the gravestones dressed in the style of a Saxon warrior. This spirit is reputed to be over 10ft tall and carries a huge sword. One local claims to have seen the enormous ghost on a cold night in October. Believing the ghost to be some sort of participant in a fancy dress costume or Hallowe'en parade, they watched in amusement until, to their horror, the ghost vanished into the north wall of the church!

Some say the ghosts at Repton are souls not at rest and have appeared more frequently since excavations at the church and surrounding area took place in the 18th century. Sir Simon Degge, travelling through Derbyshire in 1727, gives an account of an unusual story which was told to him by a local labourer and may well be connected to the giant ghost seen in the churchyard:

'About 40 years since, cutting hillocks near the surface, he met with an old stone wall. When clearing it further, he found it to be a square enclosure of 15ft. In this he found a stone coffin and saw in it the skeleton of a human body 9ft long, and round it 100 skeletons of the ordinary size, laid with the feet pointing to the coffin! The head of the great skeleton he gave to Mr Bowes, master of Repton School. I enquired of his son, one of the present masters, concerning it, but it is lost; yet, he says he remembers the skull in his father's closet, and that he often heard his father

Pears Hall, Repton. Frederick Wickham-Railton, 'the Gallery Ghost' murdered by his own brother while running the gauntlet, is still seen dashing down the corridors of Repton School. Stone steps known as 'the Devil's Leap' may also be found on the side of this building. The local legend says that if you were to jump from the top of the steps then his satanic majesty himself will appear and grant you one request in return for your mortal soul.

Repton Cross. This early market cross is the haunt of a ghostly monk. Strange orbs of light have also been seen dancing around.

mention this gigantic corpse and thinks that the skull was in proportion to a body of that stature. The present owner will not suffer it to be opened, the lady of the manor having forbidden it.'

The huge skeleton was found in a field which is now partly covered by the northern portion of the churchyard. The grave was opened again in the latter half of the 18th century, this dig revealing only a huge assortment of mixed bones.

The ghosts and strange phenomena experienced at Repton ever since seem to suggest that the disturbance of the 'giant's grave' triggered some sort of malevolent force. Perhaps the formation of the burials suggests some kind of ritualistic burying? Ancient magical practices of the entombment of the dead, with maybe equally ancient curses and magic locks to keep the dead at rest – easily disturbed, not so easily laid to rest again.

To Be or Not to Be – Superstitions

Very few of us manage to get through an average week without making some kind of reference to an ancient superstition, be it the spilling of salt, a black cat crossing our pathway or a red sky at night that heralds pleasant weather for the following day. We are all guilty of subconsciously feeding from what appears to be an almost inherent belief that simple quirks and everyday occurrences within nature can affect us in a dire and often dangerous way.

However, there are those who state that they are not, in any way, influenced by superstitious beliefs or any similar bunkum, but it may be worth remembering that not being superstitious is in itself a superstition.

Many people believe that quirks of nature, such as a flower blooming at the wrong time of year, or a comet passing through our skies, foretell events that are yet to pass, these proceedings being normally of a disastrous nature. Many believe that these beliefs are not superstitious, but are a signal by which the Almighty God communicated with man. This belief may seem a little strange to some, but for many of our forefathers it was common practice to heed the warnings which were associated with superstitions.

The following is an example of the many superstitions which are associated with the natural world:

Ass – It was once widely believed that the cross on the ass's back miraculously appeared there after an ass had carried Jesus Christ. It was further believed by many that hairs taken from the back of the animal were valuable in the concoction of cures. The animal, however, was said to be of no use afterwards.

Bats – If bats are seen to fly in circular motion after sunset, it is believed that fair and warm weather is on the way.

Cat – They were regarded by the ancient Egyptians as sacred to the Goddess Isis. We in this country have always regarded these creatures as attendants of witches. To see a black cat cross your pathway is considered by many, depending upon what part of the country you come from, to be lucky.

Mysterious big black cats seen roaming the English countryside are a fairly new phenomena. Some experts on the occult claim that the sightings of large black cats coincide with the sighting of Unidentified Flying Objects.

Death's Head Moth. According to Judaic Christian belief certain animals, birds and insects were believed to carry the souls of the dead to the 'next place', while other creatures were considered to be omens or portents of doom. The Death's Head Moth is considered by many cultures to be the ultimate harbinger of death.

Cow – If a cow turns its tail up near a hedge, it is an indication of fine weather, while cows sitting down in a field is a sure indication of ensuing rain. The cow is also sacred in Asia, where it was revered for carrying a god.

Dog – To hear a dog howling at night is a sign of bad luck. To meet a black dog on commencing a journey is also a sign of bad luck. According to gypsy law, it is incredibly unlucky if a dog digs a hole in your garden. If a strange dog follows you it is a sign of good luck, which will arrive shortly.

Fox – To see a fox is lucky, to see many is even more lucky.

Goat – This is believed by many to be one of the many forms in which Satan can appear. An old legend tells how goats are never seen for 24 hours continuously, as they have to appear in Hell so that Satan can comb their beards.

Hare – This animal was once killed by the Romans, who used its entrails to divine the future; the animal was rarely eaten. To see a hare, a rare sight these days, foretells much luck and happiness to come.

Lamb – If the first lamb of the season that you see has its head facing towards you, it is a sign of bad luck for the forthcoming year, especially if you are carrying money on your person.

Magpie – Often referred to as the 'Devil's Bird'; many people consider the bird to be an ill omen. To avert any misfortune it might be wise to whisper this ancient charm, 'I cross one magpie, one magpie crosses me. May the Devil take the magpie and God take me.' To see a magpie perched on your roof – as one of these creatures was believed to have done on Noah's Ark – shows stability.

Peacock – The feathers of a peacock are considered extremely unlucky; to have them in the house is even worse. The raucous cry of the peacock is said to signify that a storm is on the way.

Raven – This was the first bird which Noah sent out from the Ark to seek out dry land, and the bird never returned. Many people consider the bird unlucky, though in some parts of the country the opposite is maintained. Should the ravens at the Tower of London ever fly away, it is said the country will plunge into ruin. It is because of this superstition that the ravens at the Tower have had their wings clipped.

Sparrow – It is unlucky to keep a sparrow as the superstitious believe that these birds carry the souls of the dead back to heaven. Other birds were believed to carry the souls of children who were about to be born to earth; it is for this reason that the stork legend has come about.

Spider – 'If you wish to live and thrive, let the spider run alive.' So runs one jingle concerning this much superstitiously debated creature. Many people believe that the spider is a lucky omen, because one is said to have spun a web over the manger of Christ to protect him from evil. To have a small spider crawl on you, especially if it runs up your arm, is a sign of joy and prosperity.

Wasp – To kill the first wasp that you see is said to free you from your enemies for the forthcoming year.

Rabbit – The foot of a rabbit was once believed to be lucky and was carried on the person in the hope that it would ward off the evil eye. Miners are said to be very superstitious about the rabbit as to see one signifies an accident.

Snake – This is another creature which is associated with the Devil. There is a superstition that horses will not pass a snake as they can smell them.

Toad – Should the bride on her wedding day encounter a toad, it foretells of a prosperous and fertile marriage.

Etwall Lake

The name of the village of Etwall, written 'Etewelle' in the Domesday Book, is thought to be derived from Eatta Wella, meaning Eatta's water. Eatta, a Saxon headman, settled in the village in the seventh century AD. There are the remains of more than 70 wells in the grounds of the older houses in the village. Unfortunately, none of these are now in use.

Etwall is situated to the south-west of Derby, and has grown enormously since the end of World War Two, but still remains an attractive village centre.

The Parish Church of St Helen is late Perpendicular in appearance, with the large windows on the south side of the nave probably having survived from the 17th or 18th century. The church contains the canopied tomb of Sir John Port, founder of the adjacent Almshouses (known as Etwall Hospital), and of Repton School. Etwall church has a lot to offer the visitor. Inside, we encounter a fine Norman north arcade,

St Helen's Church, Etwall, haunt of the 'Crying Angel'. The tragic Green Lady of the Lake is said to be connected with the church, although her identity remains a mystery.

Etwall Lake. The haunt of a 'Green Lady' who rises from the lake covered in waterweed, deathly white, her clothes tattered and torn. She points towards the church before sinking back into the murky waters.

while the north chancel wall has a built-in stone lectern. Also in the chancel is Sir John's tomb (dated 1541). Perhaps the most fascinating feature is the Port Chapel at the east end of the north aisle.

St Helen's Church and the Sir John Port Almshouses, set on slightly rising ground, are particularly appealing. The fine wrought-iron gates by Robert Bakewell that hang outside the Almshouses, which were restored in the 1980s, add an extra touch of quality. Robert Bakewell (1682–1752), the celebrated craftsman in iron, was born at Uttoxeter. He established himself in London, filling a niche in the market conveniently vacated by the great Jean Tijou. His popularity in and around Derby seems to have resulted from a commission by Thomas Coke of Melbourne Hall. The finest collection of Bakewell ironwork is to be seen in Derby Cathedral, with its great gated screen and numerous other fittings. Disregarding his important work in private houses, other examples of his ecclesiastical craftsmanship are at Alvaston, Ashbourne, Borrowash and Duffield.

In 1970, Etwall Primary School's parent-teacher association decided to introduce the old Derbyshire custom of well dressing into the village as part of its centenary celebrations. This beautiful old custom of well dressing – or as it was once known, 'well flowering' – is very much associated with Derbyshire. It is thought to be Pagan in origin, developed from the age old fear and worship of water gods and spirits.

A prominent feature in the village is the John Port Comprehensive School, built on the site of the former Etwall Hall. The lake at John Port School is said to be haunted by a green lady who rises from the murky waters to wander the grounds. She is said to be a former servant girl from the old hall who, having been rejected in love by the Lord of the Manor, committed suicide by drowning herself in the lake. Other sources state that she is a nature spirit who presides over the sacred waters as protector and guardian.

In recent times, stories have begun to emerge of a ghostly figure that walks the graveyard in Etwall late at night. Shirley Bradshaw recounts the following strange tale...

'I was walking my dog late one evening, when I heard the sound of a woman sobbing coming from the graveyard. Thinking it was someone in mourning, I didn't really give it a moment's thought as I walked around the perimeter of the graveyard. However, as I approached, the sobbing increased and I was concerned that someone was in deep distress. I felt compelled to investigate further. Feeling protected by my dog, I walked into the graveyard. At first I could not fathom where the sound was coming from, but as I walked further I could see a figure dressed in white, standing in the far corner of the graveyard. She sounded so pitiful that I felt that I must go up to her. I approached and called out, but she didn't reply. As I came up behind her, I placed my right hand on her shoulder and as I did so she just seemed to crumble away and vanish. I stood there in shock for what seemed like an age, although it must have been just seconds. I went home a little bit wobbly from my experience and told my husband about what had taken place; he just laughed and put it down to my imagination. The strange thing is that throughout the experience my dog did not react in any way and since the event I have been told by numerous people that dogs are sensitive to ghosts, maybe it was just that the ghost wasn't a harmful one and therefore nothing to be afraid of.'

Other stories concerning Etwall churchyard relate to the Crying Angel, which stands in a lonely corner of the cemetery. This marble statue of an angel looks out sombrely onto a mixed collection of headstones. The angel is said to come alive at night and wander around, staring at the headstones. She moves in a serene way and pauses momentarily at each grave, where she cries into her hands before passing onto the next. Local school children report seeing her with outstretched wings, crying into her hands; some children dare each other to go up to the figure and touch it.

Derbyshire has other such statues that are reported to come alive; perhaps the most famous is that of Fair Flora, who can be found just outside the village of Grindleford, beside a track way branching off the B6521 road going towards Eyam. According to local legend, Flora was originally sited at Chatsworth House, but was given as a gift to the Lady of Stoke Hall. However, the Lady of the house at Stoke Hall became convinced the statue had brought bad luck and she also became frightened by it at night, so it was transferred at her insistence to

The Etwall Angel. This angel is said to come alive at night and walk the graveyard. She is often said to be seen crying as she walks among the headstones.

63

Etta's Well. The ancient art of 'well dressing' has been restored here. The waters of this well are said to have curative powers. In times past people worshipped spirits that they believed were held within the waters, and small offerings were often thrown into the wells as a sign of gratitude for the life-giving qualities the waters provided.

its present site. Many strange tales have become associated with the statue over the years. On the one hand, the statue is supposed to represent a young lady who was murdered by a jealous lover; on the other hand, the statue is said to be a memorial to a girl who drowned in the River Derwent when eloping with her lover across stepping stones above the Leadmill Bridge at Hathersage.

Calke Abbey

This charming Baroque mansion, built around 1700–04 for Sir John Harpur, is situated in the small hamlet of Calke adjacent to Ticknall village, approximately eight miles south of Derby. The interior of the building has been virtually unchanged since the late 19th century, being preserved to illustrate the decline of the English country house.

The Augustinian order of Monks built an Abbey on the site in 1133 and when the present mansion was built, it incorporated some of the mediaeval house belonging to the Augustinian canons. When the house was taken over by the National Trust in 1985, excavations revealed the remains of five adult male skeletons, which are believed to be the relics of monks from the 12th-century Abbey. Perhaps

the excavation disturbed the spirits of these religious men, as the figure of a man, dressed in a monk's cowl, has been seen wandering the outer buildings.

The most spiritually active parts of the mansion appear to be the rooms on the first floor; staff working on the ground floor have reported hearing footsteps coming from the rooms above. On investigation, the rooms were found to be empty.

Visitors to the building have also reported sightings of an old

lady in the library, who sits surveying members of the public. She is believed to be the apparition of Nanny Pearce, who looked after the children and was allowed to stay on in the building long after her services were no longer required.

A few yards away from the mansion is St Giles Church, a 19th-century building of Gothic style. Near to the church lies an area of woodland, the scene of a strange supernatural occurrence witnessed by a lady and her daughter while out walking...

'While out for a walk around the grounds of Calke Abbey, myself and my daughter had wandered into an area of woodland near to the church when I spotted a house in the distance through the trees. I decided to walk towards it for closer inspection and we began to weave our way in and out of the trees. On approaching a gate at the end of the woodland I was surprised to discover that the house was nowhere to be seen. My daughter was quite young at the time and asked in a startled voice where the house had gone. I realised that the vision had not been a figment of my imagination as my daughter had seen it too. I can find no logical explanation for what we had witnessed; it seemed that the house had simply vanished into thin air.'

Members of staff have also been on the receiving end of 'slaps' from an invisible force. Perhaps the members of the Harpur family, who were notorious for their eccentric and reclusive behaviour, still refuse to leave their home and the slaps are an expression of their annoyance at the intrusive presence of so many people!

Ministry of Angels woodcut.

Supernature

The Realm of the Fae

Spirits known as elementals are often associated with haunted stretches of woodland and rivers, mountains and valleys. Nature spirit worship was practiced by the Greeks and Romans, who believed spirits inhabited every glen, pool, and even the air.

These strange ghosts are said to be apparitions who have never existed in human form; occultists declare them to be ancient spirits. They are ruled or governed over by higher spirits such as devas or archangels, which are also known by titles such as the mighty ones. Elementals are said to predate man and fall into four categories consisting of Earth, Air, Fire and Water.

The Realm of Earth

Sometimes known collectively as gnomes, earth fae are the spiritual force of nature and reside deep within the earth – in barrows, caves, rocks and quarries. They are said to be the protectors of secret treasures hidden deep within caves beneath the earth. Brownies are one such example of these earth-loving spirits. Being small in appearance and wearing brown-coloured clothing, it is said that these mischievous spirits would attach themselves to certain families and could prove useful in menial household tasks. However, if offended, they would create poltergeist-like activity, hence why there are many stories warning to speak well of the 'little people'. In order to remove their unwanted presence, it is said that if you are to leave a brownie a new cloak and hat they would take it and never trouble you again.

The Realm of Air

Sometimes referred to as sylphs, but most often referred to as simply fairies, these elusive spirits are said to have the ability to cause storms and heavy winds, causing damage to property and disasters at sea. They often take the form, and can speak the language, of birds. These spirits who have the ability to fly are said to be the most evolved of the fae, but are also said to be the loneliest – being trapped in the space between dimensions.

The Realm of Fire

Often collectively known as salamanders, fire is a natural element which attracts numerous fairy phenomena. These spirits are temperamental in their nature and can become quite hostile if offended. Like the phoenix, their bodies are made up of living flames and they have absolute control over their own fire, burning only that which they wish to. It said that they are responsible for volcanoes erupting. It is believed by many that we each have a salamander within us throughout life, helping us to maintain body temperature and circulation.

The Realm of Water

Often referred to as undines or nymphs, these beings can be found within any body of water, from the oceans to the rivers, and from the largest lakes to the smallest rock pool. They are said to be dressed in shiny attire, their clothes changing colour, mimicking the shimmer of the water they inhabit. The undines work using the life-

giving forces and magical properties of plants, animals and also human beings. They are said to sometimes resemble humans in appearance; the legend of the mermaid is connected with these elemental beings.

If you imagine fairies you would be most likely to think of tiny creatures with cute smiles and gossamer wings fluttering among the flower beds. But according to tradition, these creatures are actually far removed from the modern-day imagery that films and cartoons create for us, like Tinkerbell from *Peter Pan* or the three fairies from *Sleeping Beauty* – Flora, Fauna and Merryweather. However, mention boggarts, bogies and banshees and can we honestly say we would imagine the same?

The Fairy Dell at Markeaton Park, site of the mysterious 'Fairy Parade'. To the upper left-hand side of this picture can be seen a strange orb. Is this possibly a fairy?

When you begin to look at the folklore of the fae, you start to discover a far more sinister world of supernatural, powerful, often harmful creatures from another dimension that somehow coincides and resides within our own.

Markeaton Fairy Dell

Markeaton Park is arguably Derby's best known and most popular park. It was officially opened by the Duke of Kent in 1931. Originally part of the Markeaton Hall Estate, owned by the Mundy family from 1516, the Hall was demolished in 1964 and was replaced by a landscaped terrace. However, the orangery still remains and is a Grade II listed building.

Despite having thousands of visitors each year, it is not commonly known that Markeaton Park is said to have its very own fairy dell.

Eleanor Griffiths, a former resident of Markeaton village, would often visit Markeaton Brook as a child.

She recollects the tale of a strange incident that happened to her in 1929 when she was just eight years old.

Eleanor, accompanied by her older sister Charlotte, set off on a warm summer's morning to paddle and catch sticklebacks in the brook. She recalls the following...

'It was a beautiful summer's day and I was paddling in the brook. Charlotte had left me momentarily to pick flowers for mother.

'I was quite happy looking among the rocks and weeds for newts and frogs, when I became aware I was being stared at.

'Looking around me, I noticed a small, withered man on the opposite bank. He couldn't have been more than 2ft tall, and was dressed in strange attire; he was wearing a blue felt hat, was barefooted and was smoking a pipe.

'Although his appearance was odd, I did not feel in the least bit frightened. Instead, a strange curiosity overtook me and I called out to him.

'He smiled and said to me in an accent I have not heard the like of since: "The parade's coming, you can't stay there long!"

'In my confusion I didn't know what to say, but remained standing in the brook. He spoke again: "Go on now, move along, or the parade can't pass!"

'I found myself stepping out of the water and climbing the bank. I turned back to the strange man and was about to question him when I heard an odd rushing sound, as if a gust of wind was approaching across the water towards me.

'Turning towards the sound, I was amazed to see several small coracle-type boats, upon which were brightly dressed pixie-like people.

'They were all singing and dancing merrily, some were playing musical instruments I didn't recognise.

'I watched as one by one the boats passed me. Some of the little people who were rowing called out and waved to me, other strange creatures danced in and around the boats accompanied by multi-coloured balls of light of differing shapes and sizes.

'All in all, it could not have lasted more than two or three minutes and once they had passed, I looked across to the opposite bank to see if the small man was still there.

'He was and smiled, lifted his felt hat as a gesture of appreciation, bowed and promptly vanished into the undergrowth.

'I felt overjoyed and couldn't wait to tell Charlotte what I had witnessed. When I did, however, Charlotte was not pleased and scolded me for telling imaginative tales!

'As the years passed, I would often visit the brook in hope of catching another glimpse of the parade, or the small strange man who had spoken to me.

'Sadly, I never did.'

The Origins of Christmas

Ever wondered about the origins of the many things we associate with Christmas? The following is an attempt to look at some of those origins. Here in Derbyshire, I am glad to say, we still carry out most of the traditional customs plus a few of our own which are peculiar to our shire.

Advent Wreath

The origins of the Advent wreath are found in the folk practices of the pre-Christian Germanic peoples, who, during the cold December darkness of Eastern Europe, gathered wreaths of evergreen and lighted fires as signs of hope in a coming spring. This practice was also carried out in order to placate their Pagan gods and appease the spirits of nature by offering them shelter for the winter.

Christians kept these popular traditions alive, and by the 1500s both Catholics and Protestants used these symbols to celebrate their Advent hope in Christ, the everlasting light.

Traditionally, the wreath is made of four candles placed in a circle of evergreens. Three candles are violet or blue (blue symbolising the hope of the season and the violet penance as in Lent) and the fourth is rose, but four white, violet, blue, or red candles can also be used. Each day at home the candles are lit, perhaps before the evening meal, one candle the first week and then another each succeeding week until 25 December. The rose candle, or joy candle, is usually lit on the third Sunday of Advent. As the candles are lit, a prayer may be said. A special fifth candle, the Christ Candle, may be placed in the centre and lit on Christmas and throughout Epiphany.

Christmas Eve

Christmas Eve, with its atmosphere of wonder, offers infinite possibilities to people's imagination. It was believed, for example, that during this magical night, sand on seashores, rocks on mountains, and the oceans and valleys all opened up in the light of the moon and the stars, to reveal the rich treasures hidden in their depths: this is the revelation of hidden treasures.

It was also said that on the stroke of midnight, farm animals acquired the marvellous and unusual gift of speech. Oxen, cows, horses, pigs and poultry began to speak to one another and to exchange strange secrets about humans, particularly their masters. Bad luck, the risk of being struck dumb or, worse still, even death, came to those who tried to spy on them. Another belief says that at midnight, farm cattle kneel in the stable to worship the infant Jesus. It is clear that these two beliefs are closely linked to the even older one that Jesus was born at midnight.

In certain parts of England and Europe there is a belief that on Christmas Eve, the dead rise up from their graves and kneel at the foot of the cemetery cross, where they are awaited by the previous parish priest wearing a white surplice and golden stole.

The priest says the prayers for the Nativity aloud and the departed respond reverently. Once the mass is finished, the dead rise, look longingly at the village and the houses where they were born, then silently return to their coffins.

Predicting the Future

On Christmas Eve, young girls would resort to certain customs to try to discover the name, or at least the initials, of their future husbands. One of these customs involved melting lead and letting it run into cold water through a key ring. From the tracery formed by the metal, girls would try to guess the initials of their future husband, as well as his profession, his personality, or his looks. A third practice was to peel an apple, being careful to keep the peel in a single continuous ribbon. Then the peel would be re-formed as closely as possible to look like the original apple. The peel would then be thrown on the floor from above the girl's head. She could then discover the initials of her future spouse from the design that the peel made on the floor.

Origins

Before Christianity, there were many Pagan religious festivals around 25 December. The best known were those of Saturnalia, from 17 to 24 December; the cult of Mithras, which is celebrated on 25 December; and the festival of the Sigillaria at the end of December.

The cult of Mithras came from Persia and spread during the third and fourth centuries BC. The cult has many similarities with Christian ceremonies and rites including baptism, communion wafer and Sunday rest.

On 25 December the sacrifice of a bull celebrated the *Sol invictus* (the invincible sun) and signalled the birth of a young sun god who sprang from a rock or a cave in the form of a new-born infant.

The festival of the Sigillaria, or terracotta seals, was a Pagan Roman holiday. At the end of Saturnalia, Romans used to give gifts, especially to children – rings, seals and tiny objects. This festival was the time for great feasts, during which houses were decorated with green plants.

Hanging Stockings

The custom of hanging stockings comes from England. Father Christmas once dropped some gold coins while coming down the chimney; the coins would have fallen through the ash grate and been lost if they hadn't landed in a stocking that had been hung out to dry. Since that time, children have continued to hang out stockings in hopes of finding them filled with gifts.

Actually, the hanging of stockings by the fire supposedly dates back to the actual Saint Nicholas, a bishop in Lycia in Asia Minor (present-day Turkey) during the fourth century AD. According to the legend, there was a poor man with three daughters who could not provide a dowry for them to be married. One night, Nicholas secretly dropped a bag of gold into an open window of the house. The oldest daughter was then allowed to be married. This was repeated later with the second daughter. Finally, determined to uncover his benefactor, the father secretly hid each evening by his third daughter's window until he caught the saint tossing in a bag of gold. Nicholas begged the man to not reveal what he had done, not wanting to bring attention to himself. Word got out anyway, and when anyone received a gift from an unknown source, it was attributed to Saint Nicholas. The stockings later came into play in one legend, when the third daughter had hung her stockings by the fire to dry them out after washing them, so when St Nicholas tossed in the bag of gold, it landed in one of the stockings. Thus the tradition began.

Greenery

The hanging of greenery around the house, such as holly and ivy, is a winter tradition with origins well before the Christian era. Greenery was brought into the house to lift sagging winter spirits and remind people that spring was not far away. The needle-like points of holly leaves are thought by some to resemble the crown of thorns that

Jesus wore when he was crucified. The red berries may symbolise the drops of blood he shed.

Mistletoe, also known as thunder blossom, is found on willow and apple trees (occasionally oak); the practice of hanging it in the house goes back to the times of the ancient Druids. It is supposed to possess mystical powers that bring good luck to the household and ward off evil spirits.

Christmas Tree

The fir tree has a long association with Christianity. It began in Germany almost 1,000 years ago when St Boniface, who converted the German people to Christianity, was said to have come across a group of Pagans about to sacrifice a young boy while worshipping an oak tree. In anger, St Boniface is said to have cut down the oak tree and, to his amazement, a young fir tree sprung up from the roots of the oak tree. St Boniface took this as a sign of the Christian faith. It was not until the 16th century that fir trees were brought indoors at Christmas time. The decorating of Christmas trees, though primarily a German custom, has been widely popular in England since 1841 when Prince Albert had a Christmas tree set up in Windsor Castle for Queen Victoria and their children. At that time, the tree would have been decorated with candles to represent stars, but because of the danger of fire, an American telephonist invented the electric Christmas lights we know today.

The Yule Log

The yule log was originally an entire tree, carefully chosen and brought into the house with great ceremony. The large end would be placed into the hearth while the rest of the tree stuck out into the room. The log would be lit from the remains of the previous year's log which had been carefully stored away and slowly fed into the fire through the 12 days of festivities. Having the remains of the yule log in the house throughout the year was thought to give protection against fire and it was considered important that someone with clean hands carry out the re-lighting process . Nowadays of course, most people have central heating so it is very difficult to burn a tree!

Christmas Crackers

These were conceived in 1850 by a London confectioner called Tom Smith, while sitting in front of his log fire. His attention was focused on the sparks and cracks emanating from the flames when, suddenly, he thought what an added attraction it would be if his sweets and toys could be revealed with a crack when their fancy wrappings were pulled in half. Today's crackers are short cardboard tubes wrapped in colourful paper and traditionally there is one cracker next to each plate on the Christmas dinner table. When the crackers are pulled, out falls a colourful party hat, a toy or a gift and a festive joke. The party hats look like crowns and we assume these symbolise the crowns worn by the three kings.

Christmas Pudding

Over the years many superstitions have surrounded this popular festive dessert. It is said that puddings should be made by the 25th Sunday after Trinity, prepared with 13 ingredients to represent Christ and his disciples, and that every member of the family take turns to stir the pudding with a wooden spoon from east to west, in honour of the three kings.

Putting a silver coin in the pudding is another age-old custom that is said to bring wealth, health and happiness to whoever finds it. Other items put in the mixture over the years include rings, which mean marriage within a year, and thimbles and buttons, which predict the finders will remain spinsters and bachelors.

Life before life? Reincarnation

'In the beginning, before the time of man, there existed in the universe beings which were androgynous. These beings were without need as we know it; being totally at one with themselves, they needed no other stimuli to exist. Being both able to reproduce by themselves and having no determined length of time in which to exist and die, they subsisted in total bliss. The gods in that time watched the creatures closely and eventually became envious of their total completeness. Becoming angered by these beings' unique oneness, the gods split them in two, cast them down to this world, bound them in flesh and, from that day to this, those beings — us — seek to find that which we were divided from. Forever seeking our other halves, forever asking ourselves when we meet potential partners, "Is this the one?" When we eventually find that which we were divided from, we will become whole again, thus allowing ourselves to pass on to a spiritual dimension where we may once again exist in total bliss.'

So reads one of the many legends associated with reincarnation. Although this may be a simple way of looking at the subject – and admittedly rather a romantic one – the issue of reincarnation and what it means is a great deal more complex, surrounded by much mystery, argument and debate.

Throughout the world belief in reincarnation appears to be growing. Our ancient Celtic ancestors dwelling in Derbyshire would almost certainly have believed in the often religious doctrine that the souls of humans, as well as animals, had the ability to transmigrate, at the point of death, from one biological form to be reborn in another. It was believed in ancient Celtic mythology that the corpses of slain warriors were cast into a cauldron of rebirth from which they arose, refreshed and ready once again to do battle with their enemies. These beliefs would almost certainly have been held by the ancient Celts of Derbyshire. Indeed, throughout the world, in nearly all spiritual and religious backgrounds (especially Hinduism and Buddhism), we find the belief in continuous life cycles common.

In Christianity, the belief in reincarnation was at one time a strong one until, in the sixth century, the Emperor Justinian issued 15 'anathemas' – formal ecclesiastical curses involving ex-communication – which condemned the idea of reincarnation. The Christian church appears to have deplored the idea ever since, even though they believe their prophet and son of God, Jesus of Nazareth, himself rose from the dead.

Many modern hypnotherapists claim to have the ability to access previous lives through a series of suggestive phrases and words which soothe the conscious mind – allowing a doorway to our past lives to be opened. In this semi-conscious state, we are sometimes allowed to glimpse images of lives past. Many books presently abound in the market concerning alleged regressed individuals, who claim to have verified their past lives through intensive and thorough historical research.

Most people, at some time or another, have experienced the strange feeling of déjà vu, which is a feeling of having already experienced the present situation, such as knowing what to expect further along a country road not journeyed previously. These types of occurrences are not uncommon and there are several theories as to why these feelings of familiarity happen to many people on a frequent basis. Many of us are familiar with people who claim to have been Napoleon or Cleopatra or another famous historical figure in a previous lifetime. While we are inclined to scoff at such claims, often believing these people to be unbalanced, it is worth remembering that we cannot disprove these claims (as we equally cannot prove that they are true), even if the individuals concerned are decidedly odd.

Scientists claim that the human mind is capable of convincing us that we are experiencing memories from a past lifetime, when what we are actually perceiving is only a regurgitation of an article or book, or other visual stimulation we have experienced years or even decades before. This process, known as cryptomnesia, (remembering things once forgotten) is currently under investigation and research in universities and medical centres throughout the world. Another scientific belief is that of genetic memory, where it may be possible for memories of our ancestors to be contained within our genetic make-up and perhaps stored in areas of our brains not yet fully understood. When a series of events takes place similar to memories genetically stored, our conscious mind reactivates our inherited experiences, allowing us to believe that we have undergone an incident, or relived a memory, from a life lived before. What we may have experienced, however, is a memory gone through and genetically recorded by a great-great-great-grandparent.

However, the mystically and spiritually inclined accept the concept of reincarnation, claiming that we are continuously reborn as part of a spiritual learning process. When we have learned all that is necessary to have advanced our souls to a state of reasonable divine purity, we can at last pass on to another higher level of spirituality for ever.

Life before life, reincarnation. Can souls survive the death process and then transmigrate into another form? Many world religions believe that they can. There are accounts of thousands of people who claim to have existed in a previous life.

Feast for the Dead

There was a time when the very mention of All Hallows Eve struck terror into the hearts of men and women. Now, most people view the annual celebration with little or no fear at all.

Hallowe'en is, to most of us, a time of merriment and fun, a time for children to dress in ghoulish costumes and knock on doors trick-or-treating, with a look of expectation on their faces. Later they return home and marvel at their booty, and relate scary tales and ghost stories to one another.

How many of those fun-seeking youngsters realise that the true origins of Hallowe'en are both sinister and complex?

To many Pagans, 31 October is Samhain and is a particularly important time of the year, when the two worlds – those of the living and the dead – are thought to be near each other. There are four great Sabbaths and four lesser Sabbaths, referred to as Escatts, in the Pagan year. Hallowe'en is perhaps the most important.

This time of year also marked the end of summer and the beginning of winter. The ancient Celts only recognised those two seasons. Huge bonfires would be lit on hillsides across England and the spirits of the dead were encouraged to find their way back to this world.

To ancient man, Hallowe'en was a time of worship and adoration of those gone before us. Food was left out in large quantities, wine and alcohol was freely available and music, dancing and loud celebrations took place. Celtic people believed that death was just another stage of life. They believed that all souls, after death, entered a giant cauldron, from which they one day would be born again. Reincarnation was an integral part of their belief system.

Contrary to popular belief, Hallowe'en was, in fact, never a sombre or grim occasion to Pagans, but a time of cheerful merriment, remembrance and goodwill – a time to honour and worship the dead.

Candles were once placed in windows to guide the souls of the departed back home. This practice is still common in many parts of the British Isles. Another ancient practice was to leave food and wine on the table and a fire in the hearth before retiring to bed. To offer the dead food and warmth would surely bring favourable fortune to the household throughout the forthcoming year.

Here in Derbyshire things are no different to anywhere else in England. Children still dress up in their costumes, going from house to house and generally having a great time. The practice of dressing up in costumes is not an entirely new concept. It derives from an ancient practice when men believed that to dress in such a way would enable them to go unnoticed by evil forces out to do harm. Derbyshire's ancient dwellers had no doubts that elves, pixies, fairies, goblins and demons existed, or that the dead walked the earth.

Special services were once held by the Christian Church at this time of year to bless its congregation in a bid to keep evil forces at bay. Bells were rung throughout towns and villages and holy water was sprinkled on the doorsteps of houses.

Finally, for those who carve faces in pumpkins to place on dark windowsills, it is worth remembering that this was once done to attract the spirits of the dead. The grim faces were carved in an attempt to ward off evil spirits, while the flame that burned within was intended to light the way. Beware...!

Pumpkins. The grotesque faces carved upon pumpkins was originally an attempt to ward off evil spirits, while the flame that burned within was intended to light the way for the souls of the departed back to earth, thus allowing us to celebrate those whom we have lost.

The Magic of Hallowe'en

Love Apple Charm

At midnight, take a large red apple and peel it with a black-handled knife so that the peel forms one continuous coil.

Then, stand facing a large mirror in a room lit by the flame of a virgin white candle. Holding the peel in the left hand (the hand traditionally said to be linked directly to the heart), turn three times then cast the peel over the right shoulder.

Behold! The skin will fall to the floor, forming the initials of your true love. Should the skin break into many pieces, the outlook is considered to be gloomy.

A word of warning – do not look into the mirror after the peel has been thrown, as you may see reflected there a face that is not of this world.

This charm can also be used at Christmas to predict the future.

The Clay Charm

Take four pieces of white paper and write the names of three admirers in blood-red ink on three of them. Roll the pieces of paper into small balls and next encase them within wet clay.

Place the clay balls in a bowl of water into which you have first added a handful of salt. Then place the bowl underneath or near to your bed.

In the morning, one of the clay balls will have released its contents – the name written on the floating piece of paper will be the name of the lover that you will marry.

Should the blank piece of paper be the only one floating then you are yet to meet your true love.

A similar charm involves writing the letters of the alphabet on small pieces of cardboard before placing them face down into a bucket of water. In the morning, check to see which pieces have turned over during the night. These letters will spell the name of your true love.

Evil Eye Charm

For those who still believe in the evil eye, think that they may have been cursed, or just want to change their luck for the better, the following charm will promote good fortune and keep evil away.

On the evening of Hallowe'en, take an egg, the shell of which should be as light as possible – white being the best – and draw upon it the universal antidote against evil – the Cross.

Next, carefully carry the egg into the garden and deposit it into a shallow grave. Spit into the hole and rapidly fill it in. Then walk away and forget about it. Your luck is sure to change for the better.

The Apple Twig Charm

According to some, this next charm is a very potent one.

Before midnight has struck on All Hallows Eve, take a black-handled knife and go to an apple tree. From the tree, cut three short twigs and carry them back indoors. Should you have mistletoe growing nearby this is even better and adds to the potency.

Next, tie the twigs or mistletoe with red thread wrapped three times about them, and then place them under your bed. Then, take a candle and stick three pins into it while repeating this charm,

> *'It's not the candle alone I stick*
> *But my would-be lover's heart I prick;*
> *Be he asleep or be he awake,*
> *A vision of him this night I call to make.'*

Burn the candle for an hour then extinguish the flame. Within the next three nights you will dream of the one you will marry.

Ghostly Black Dogs

Sightings of phantom black dogs are numerous throughout Britain, and virtually every area has its own variant. Barguest, Shriker, Guytrash, Black Shuck and Wish Hounds are just a few names given to such apparitions. Various gods associated with the underworld, hunting, birth and death are also connected with these dogs, such as Hecate, Diana and Artemis. There is also the story of Gabriel Ratchet's hounds, which are said to race across the night skies chasing human souls condemned to hell for eternity.

Black dogs seem to haunt ancient lanes, crossroads, areas of woodland and churchyards. The haunts of these phantom hounds are also said to denote ley lines, Derby being believed to lie directly within such an earth power grid system.

Derbyshire has many reported sightings, mostly in close proximity to graveyards, woods and crossroads. The Church Grim, as it is called, has been sighted near to St Peter's Church in Chellaston. According to folklore, the first person to be buried in a churchyard was believed to return as a ghost in order to

Chellaston alabaster pit. Once famous for its alabaster mining, the now overgrown pits are haunted by a ghostly black dog, which has also been seen in St Peter's churchyard. According to folklore, this ghostly apparition was known as the Church Grim and was said to be a harbinger of terrible events yet to happen.

guard the site against the Devil. Due to this concern, a black dog was often buried before any human in order to guard the dead. Many believe that the sightings of these phantom black dogs in and around graveyards are the ghosts of these guarding dogs. The apparition seen in Chellaston is reported to be a huge, bear-like creature, with a dirty, matted coat. It seems to appear from thin air and walks silently in and around the graveyard, often pausing to survey its witnesses with large, saucer-like glowing eyes before vanishing again.

Within a few yards of St Peter's Church lies the remains of the alabaster mines in a small area of woodland. Chellaston became famous in mediaeval times for the white alabaster quarried there. The quarries were re-opened in Victorian times when alabaster was used for figure carving. Many examples of such carvings can be found across the Midlands and within several Derby churches. Remains of the quarries can clearly be seen among the woodland and children use the dug-out areas of earth as a playground. Sightings of the phantom black dog have been reported in this area.

Simon Maddon recounts the following tale...

'As a child I used to stay with my cousins, who lived in Chellaston, every weekend. On Sunday afternoons we would take our bikes up to the woods behind Pit Close Lane and ride in and out of the dug-out remains of the alabaster mines. One afternoon it was raining particularly hard and I had fallen off my bike several times in the mud. Tired of being ridiculed, I took off on my own deeper into the woodland. Suddenly, I had an overwhelming feeling that I was being watched. I turned to see a huge hound with a long, black, shaggy coat. It was much bigger than any dog I have ever seen and I instantly felt uneasy. It stood staring at me for what seemed like an eternity, but could only have been a few seconds, before suddenly setting off along the path towards me. I was only a small boy at the time and was frightened that the dog was about to attack, but it ran straight past me through the trees and out into the flat, grassy area beyond. I don't know why I felt the need to follow it, but I turned my bike around and did so. However, when I rode out between the trees onto the flat area beyond, the dog was nowhere to be seen. It was if it had vanished. I was shaken by the incident for some time afterwards and the following weekend I mentioned the incident to my uncle. I was surprised that he didn't tell me off for inventing far-fetched stories, instead he informed me that several people had witnessed similar incidents around the same area.'

Burial mound trees. Derbyshire has a wealth of ancient artefacts. Trees were once sacred to Pagans and Druids. Believing that spirits resided in the tree, they would make offerings of food to placate the spirit in the hope that it would bring them good fortune.

Haunted Trees

Trees have always played an important part in world religions. References include the Bo tree, under which the great Buddha sat, the spectacular Yggdrasil of Norse mythology, upon which the god Odin hung and spied the runes, the barren fig tree, which Jesus of Nazareth cursed, and, of course, the Elder Tree upon which Judas later hanged himself.

The Druids were said to worship trees and were known as the keepers of the old religion. Their temples were the sacred oak groves, and they believed that all things in creation harboured the spirits of their dead ancestors as well as elemental spirits of nature. The very word 'Druid' is said to translate into 'knowing the oak tree' and the word 'derwent', so common in Derbyshire, means 'abundant in oaks'. The chieftain trees which the Druids worshipped were the oak, apple, rowan, willow, ash, beech and birch. These Celtic beliefs were at one time so widely believed that the Council of Tours in 567 declared that those who 'worshipped trees, stones or fountains' should be excommunicated.

Today there is very little left of the ancient groves and mystical trees which once scattered the face of Derbyshire, apart from a few random trees which have at some point been said to be haunted by phantoms, spirits of nature and the little people of folklore and legend.

Derbyshire's most famous tree was undoubtedly a great oak which once resided at the Hagge, a 16th-century building, now a farmhouse, west of Staveley at Nether Handley. The tree was known as the mandrake tree, or the haunted oak, and was believed to be the only tree in the area that bore mistletoe. This tree was always venerated by the local people, who believed it to have healing powers. A macabre feature of the tree was that it was said to bleed if ever it was cut, and anyone that was foolish enough to damage the tree was terrified by a blood-curdling, half-human scream, which the tree emitted. The tree eventually blew down in a fearsome storm on 12 December 1883 – it was believed at that time to be 360 years old.

Another vanished tree, which was said to have the ability to foretell future events, once existed in the grounds of Hassop Hall near Bakewell. The tree, a beech, was believed to whisper the rightful ownership of the Hassop estates, which was at one time the subject of much debate. When the wind blew from the west, stirring the leaves of the tree, it could clearly be heard to whisper 'All hail, true heir, that stills my voice.' Local legend tells the story that several owners of the hall attempted to cut the tree down, but, no sooner had the axe been lifted, than the would-be destroyer met with some unfortunate accident.

Another ancient tree still living, this time a yew, is said to be haunted by several ghosts which have been periodically seen over the last century, including the ghost of a peddler who was murdered a mere 150 yards from the yew. The tree is perhaps one of the oldest in England and is thought to be over 2,000 years old, but is more likely to date from Romano-British or Saxon times, when the area of the tree could have been a cult centre.

Other trees in Derbyshire include the Doveridge yew, under whose branches Robin Hood and Maid Marian were said to have been married, and where the ghost of a green man is frequently seen. A talking tree at Allestree in Derby and an ancient oak tree that moves its location can also be found close to the banks of the River Derwent at Darley Abbey.

If you wish to see two spectacular examples of haunted trees, you need go no further than Wingfield Manor and Long Lane at Thurvaston. Both these trees have an aesthetically haunting charisma. The former is believed to have grown from a walnut, which Anthony Babington dropped while sneaking into Wingfield Manor, having fallen in love with the ill-fated Mary, Queen of Scots – a love which inevitably led to both their executions. The latter is a fine example of a revered tree which, for centuries, appears to have been a local convergence point for the community. In times past, the oak, which finally expired in 1929 at The Stoop in Thurvaston, was often garlanded on special occasions. The owner, Mr J. Hunt, stated that there were many strange stories about the tree, none of which he was prepared to tell. However, upon this once great oak and within the contorted swirls and curves of the rotting bark, you can see all manner of strange and wonderful faces – perhaps of spirits still held there. The best one is clearly the profile of a bearded man, which consumes the upper portions of the tree, looking curiously like a Druid.

Another unusual tree, known as the Witch's Tree, can be found at Shardlow, not far from a place called Ridings Hill, which stands on higher ground than the surrounding area between the flood plains of the Trent and Mersey Canal and the River Trent. The area was once known as Dead Man's Drop, as a gibbet

Lone Tree. This enigmatic tree standing on the weaver hills and overlooking Derby and Derbyshire is believed by some to grant wishes. The tree is furthermore said to be a focal point for fairy gatherings, and strange glowing balls of light and wispy smoke are said to be common phenomena here.

had once stood about 80 yards away from where the solitary oak tree can be found.

When construction began on the A50, rumours began to circulate concerning strange flashing lights and mysterious cloaked figures being seen in the area. The Witch's Tree stood with many other trees, which were all pulled out, but they strangely left the oak tree alone. According to local legend, the tree was the final resting place of a witch who had been buried beneath it in the belief that her spirit would enter into the tree and no longer continue to influence its evil upon innocent people – perhaps she had been executed at the gibbet?

A building that had once been a communal milking barn was demolished and beneath the foundations were discovered two skeletons, which both had their hands and heads cut off. Were these remains interred in this way in the ancient belief that to cut off the hands and head of a witch or evil sorcerer was the universal antidote against them coming back from the grave to haunt the living?

So superstitious were the workmen about the Witch's Tree and its curse that they refused to dig it out despite the loss of over 11,000 tons of gravel. The tree remains to this day and is still said to be the haunt of the witch that is buried beneath it. She can be seen on dark nights cloaked in rags, her hair matted, her body twisted, wandering the area in search of souls to drag down into the darkest recesses of hell, there to be tormented by demons for all eternity.

Fairy thorn trees. Thorn trees, or hawthorns, are a common sight around Derby. Farmers often leave these trees untouched as to cut one down and destroy it is to bring disaster to the farm and the forthcoming harvest. Thorn trees were once believed to be gathering places for the 'little people'

Granny Knows Best

Before the time of organised medicine, there existed a very different method of receiving medical treatments and cures. No matter what the ailment or disease, there was sure to be some concoction of herbs, powders or potion that would guarantee a remedy.

In old Derbyshire books and manuscripts there can be found numerous references to cures that seem strange and bizarre by today's standards.

It seems that many of the cures are surrounded by elements of magic and mysticism. Perhaps this is because man, in his inconsistent knowledge, sought the help of ancient spirits of healing to bring about a better cure.

Perhaps it was ignorance, or could it just be that the ancient soothsayers and healers knew more than we credit them for?

In certain parts of the county, it was believed at one time that people and animals could be cursed or have the evil eye put upon them by an ill-wishing neighbour or enemy.

In many parts of Derbyshire and the Peak District, it was common to find items such as animal skulls and even painted eyes placed above doors and windows of houses in a bid to avert the evil eye.

This practice continues to this day, but the eyes and skulls have been replaced by horseshoes.

One has only to look at many of the older farmhouses in the county to see that such trees as holly and yew have been planted beside the doors. This was done in the hope that evil and bad luck would be averted. The holly and the yew tree are prime examples of trees that were believed to have magical powers – both symbolise long life and prosperity.

When people fell ill, there was often no alternative but to visit a wise man or woman. Most villages had one, although with the onslaught of witch hunts and persecution trials of anyone vaguely associated with magic, local healers and sages went underground and became rare.

Nevertheless, the practice of going to see a healer continued. Anything could be treated, from head lice to the plague. There was a cure for nearly everything and, if the herbs and potions failed, it was often blamed on black magic.

In Eyam, when the Black Death raged in 1665, there sprang up a whole series of strange and peculiar healing remedies.

We may look back and smile at their use of common vegetables, tomatoes, fruits and nettles to heal the plague but, to the people living at the time, such cures seemed very possible and were their best hope.

Another strange cure for the plague was based on warm beer, into which would be infused herbs which had been picked at an exact astrological moment. All herbs and plants were at one time assigned to an astrological planet.

Urine seemed to be one of the most frequently used granny cures. Stale or fresh, urine was thought to be all-healing, having at some point been used to treat most exterior conditions and, on occasion, internal ones.

Gold, too, appears to have had a great deal of medicinal value, especially to treat exterior conditions of the skin, such as warts and blemishes.

Then there was the crucifix, which was used as an external antidote against most illnesses. The practice of carrying a crucifix or cross was often not just for religious or pious purposes. It was commonly believed that some illnesses were brought about by little demons that entered the body, making the person ill.

Even today, in some religions and doctrines it is thought that devils possess people, causing them to be unwell. Healing ceremonies and minor exorcisms are still carried out in the hope that the demon causing the affliction will be driven out and the patient healed.

Herbs appear to play the greatest part in cures. Today's herbal cures are nearly all based on earlier discoveries.

Modern medicine also owes much to ancient granny cures and many drugs are directly derived from herbs.

Although many drugs on the market today are synthetic, having been clinically tested, approved and finally released for use by the public, many medicines still owe much to granny cures, which kept the practice of treating ailments with herbs and spices alive.

Vampires –

Folklore or Fact?

Rising from their cold, dark graves to suck the blood of mortals, vampires kill indiscriminately and care little for human emotions. There was a time when such creatures were believed to wander the earth, seeking to destroy all human life. Today the debate continues:

There are those who believe they are living vampires, and those who study and discuss vampire fiction and folklore. For decades, folklorists and vampirologists have been busy studying the universal spread of the vampire – every culture has a vampire of its own.

Vampires are identified in every aspect of myth and folklore. There are undead vampires, supernatural vampires, vampire deities, vampire demons, vampire spirits, vampire animals, living vampires and psychic vampires.

Anything that returns from the dead, that is not human but desires sex from humans, kills people in the night and seems interested in blood is labelled a vampire. Ghouls, gods, succubi (demons that sleep with humans), psychopaths, devils and witches all are crowded under the same heading. They're all vampires, but for different reasons.

When living people call themselves real vampires and attempt to define what they mean by the word, they are usually unable to do so with any great clarity. Real vampires may be blood drinkers or psychic vampires, they may be turned after being born human or be born a vampire.

Depending on which source you read, real vampires may be inheritors, classical, viral or just 'wannabes'. Ultimately, the definition of a vampire seems to be open to interpretation. Above all, they are a mystery: myths, legends, folklore, unknown knowledge, untold stories.

We are most familiar with the Hollywood portrayal of the dark classic vampire. We have grown to love and hate them at the same time. But research shows that the

dark classic vampire is nothing more than a collection of inspired, attention-grabbing creations and a betrayal of what vampires really are.

Here in Derbyshire, we have numerous stories of these creatures stalking in the shadows in search of victims. Some say the reason that vagrants are scarce in the county is because of the presence of vampires.

Derby's most famous vampire is the Black Death Vampire. The Black Death struck the town in 1349, and more people died in St Peter's Parish than in any other part of Derby. From a population of 3,000, one third died from the Black Death.

One of the symptoms of the plague was a coma or deep sleep. With so many people dying, it was quite common for people who were still alive to be brought out to the funerary collector and taken directly to their place of burial.

There were several reports of people being buried alive, and frantically trying to claw their way out of their coffins. These incidents gave rise to speculation that the plague was sent by Satan and that these poor unfortunates were vampires – the dead rising.

Because of the vast number of plague victims, space for burials began to run out. Once church graveyards were full, people were buried on the outskirts of town. One such burial ground existed at what is now known as Deadman's Lane, which runs between Osmaston Road and London Road. There is a reported sighting, at the bottom of nearby Ascot Drive, of a vampire who is accompanied by the smell of rotting fruit.

Strangely enough, the very first public showing anywhere in the world of Hamilton Deane's stage adaptation of Bram Stoker's *Dracula* was performed at Derby at the Grand Theatre on 15 May 1924. Stories soon began to circulate about vampires walking the alleys and streets of Derby at night and very few people ventured outside their houses after nightfall.

Other areas of Derbyshire that have local vampires are Beeley Moor near Chatsworth House, Stanton Moor and several places around Ashbourne, especially the town centre.

Spirits of Nature

There are many local legends of people seeing strange creatures, ghosts, goblins, fairies and water spirits and so on, in our shire. For generations, people have believed that such creatures exist and to disturb or in any way upset one of them, by cutting a sacred tree down or by building a wall across an ancient fairy dell, would inevitably bring about ruin. Farmers were especially wary of nature spirits, and in times past would often plant holly, rowan or thorn trees, which were believed to have magical powers and would protect the house from these mischievous spirits.

Today we may scoff at the idea of a spirit residing in a tree, a cave, a stretch of water or a well, but to ancient man residing in the valleys and forests of our shire, these creatures of antiquity and nature were very real. Many people believed that the Green Man of legend (Robin Hood) is entirely indigenous to Nottinghamshire when, in fact, there are reports of him in nearly all the counties in the East Midlands. Some historians, and nearly all those that research the occult and Celtic legend, agree that green men (as they have now become known) are almost certainly a representation of an ancient fertility god representing the cycle of death to the birth of new life – the death of winter and the birth of spring. He was also known as the

Man O' Green. A carving of a 'Green Man' or 'Man O' Green'. His image can be found on Derby Cathedral as well as on churches across Derbyshire. Many historians believe that his figure is a representation of an ancient fertility god, representing the cycle of death to the birth of new life; the death of winter and the birth of spring.

King of May, Jack in the Green, Father of the Wood and Robin of the Hood, and recognised throughout Europe; the French called him '*tête de feuilles*' (head of leaves) and the Germans called him 'Blattmaske' (leaf mask). He is still recognised and celebrated today within Derbyshire; the Garland festival is held in Castleton, in which the leading character (referred to as a Jack in the Green) wears a hollow frame covered with leaves and flowers.

As the peoples of our country rapidly became Christianised, they adapted older beliefs into the new doctrines and, not content to entirely let go of the old ways, incorporated many of their mythical figures into the fabric of their churches. We need only to look at many of our present-day churches that have survived from the 14th, 15th and 16th century to see that the people who designed and built them still partly believed in the Celtic Gods and spirits.

Many churches still have an abundance of carved stone heads. Green Men are normally shown with leaves coming out of their mouths. Their images can also be found on cathedrals and churches that date from as far back as the 11th century, usually carved from stone and high on buildings. Shiela-na-Gigs (goddesses of fertility) can also be found within Derbyshire; two examples are a carving seen inside the old stables at Haddon Hall, and another within the parish church at Melbourne. Other various stone carvings such as gargoyles, horned men, mouth pullers, dragons and strange animals are all perhaps representations of almost forgotten gods and goddesses.

Our ancestors also knew the value of clean water; it is rumoured that they often

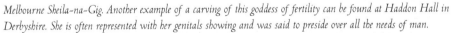

Melbourne Sheila-na-Gig. Another example of a carving of this goddess of fertility can be found at Haddon Hall in Derbyshire. She is often represented with her genitals showing and was said to preside over all the needs of man.

sacrificed a young virgin to placate the earth gods and goddesses. Many serious investigators of the paranormal have pondered why there seem to be so many reported incidents of white ladies haunting the countryside and ancient places. Perhaps this is because so many young virgins were sacrificed to river gods and are bound by Druidical magic to protect the place that they gave up their lives for.

Most wells and water stretches seem to be haunted by their own personal ghosts. Many rivers are also said to harbour spirits of nature and in some parts of England it was not uncommon, at certain times of the year, for locals to make special trips to certain stretches of water to drink from them, believing that at strategic points within a year the water was imbued with miraculous healing powers.

These beliefs, once again, appear to descend from our ancestors, who made comparisons with natural phenomena in nature and human anatomy. Certain rivers and water stretches are, at times, known to change colour from yellow ochre to brown and red, when there has been heavy rain and flooding. Superstitious people often believed that when the water changed colour it was a sign of a magical transformation, which the spirits of the water, or the gods, were allowing to happen for fertility purposes. So a river turning red, from flooding water running through a clay bed further upriver, was often thought to represent the fact that a god had allowed its own blood to mingle with the waters, thus reinforcing the life-giving qualities of the water with the god's own life force. Others believed that the river turning reddish or brown was an indication of the Earth Mother (or Goddess of Nature) menstruating, while others believed it to be an omen of misfortune and an indication that those who were once sacrificed to the waters were reminding all of their presence through the ghostly transformation of the water.

The Worlds Within

Dale Abbey

In 1155, Serlo de Grendon, Lord of the Dale, invited some Austin canons from Calke Abbey to establish a colony at Depedale, as the area of Dale Abbey was then known.

The Abbey became successful but, after several years, the canons became more obsessed with themselves than their spirituality and the improvement of their minds. The King came to know of their transgressions and ordered them to leave on account of their hunting. They resigned and returned to Calke Abbey.

For some time the priory remained closed until William de Grendon, son of Serlo, invited another group of canons, from the Abbey of Tupholme in Lincolnshire, to establish a fresh community at Dale. The new canons only stayed for seven years.

When the priory was eventually given up, Henry, the prior, refused to leave. It was discovered that he had been involved in counterfeiting money, and that he had had a relationship with a working girl from Morley, in whose company he was eventually found. He was taken by force back to Tupholme and, not long after, he committed suicide by cutting his wrists while taking a hot bath.

After another unsuccessful attempt to establish an Abbey at Dale, Geoffrey de Salicosa Mara and his wife, Matilda, gave the village of Stanley to the Premonstratensian Order and joined it with Dale, thus making it financially stronger. Under the guidance of the new Abbott, the Abbey became well established and, by the time of the Dissolution, it was one of the most successful abbeys in England.

The story of the ghost of Dale Abbey begins more than 800 years ago. An ancient manuscript by a canon named Thomas de Muscova, now in the British Museum, chronicles the history of Dale Abbey, including the events of the life of a Derby baker, who, for many years, gave presents of food from the Church of St Mary's to the poor.

One night, in a dream, the Blessed Virgin Mary appeared to the baker and said:

'Acceptable in the eyes of my son and of me, are the alms thou hast bestowed. But now, if thou art willing to be made perfect, leave all thou hast and go to Depedale where thou shalt serve my son and me in solitude and when thou shalt happily terminated thy course, thou shalt inherit the Kingdom of love, joy and eternal bliss which God has prepared for those who love him.'

When the baker awoke, he set out to look for Depedale. He came to the village of Stanley, where he heard a woman say to her daughter, 'Take our calves with you,

drive them as far as Depedale and make haste back.' The baker felt that God was indirectly telling him which way to go, so he followed the young maiden to Depedale and eventually came across a sandstone hillside. He carved himself a dwelling in the rock and became a hermit.

Some weeks after the baker had made his home in the cave, Ralph Fitz Geremund, the Lord of Ockbrook and

Dale Abbey arch. All that remains of the Abbey is this beautiful great chancel arch. The sounds of chanting have been reportedly heard in this area and the figure of a hooded monk has been seen standing near the arch. This ghostly monk is believed to be the same apparition that haunts the hermit's cave.

Alvaston, was hunting deer when he saw smoke coming from the hermit's cave. He was angry that anyone should dare to live in Depedale without his permission, the penalties being severe for anyone who broke them. On reaching the cave he found the hermit dressed in rags of sackcloth and animal skins. Lord Geremund demanded to know why the hermit was trespassing on his property. When he heard the explanation he became moved by the story and granted him the site of his cell, as well as the tithe of a mill at Alvaston, which would support him in his spiritual quest. Shortly after being granted the mill, the hermit began to build himself a chapel and oratory near a spring, westward of the cave he had cut for himself.

Several decades after the hermit had built his oratory, which eventually became a monastery, a notorious highway robber named Uthlagus happened to be passing with his band of outlaws. Deciding to settle for the night on top of the hill where the hermit's cave was, it was not long before they all fell fast asleep. During the night, Uthlagus had a dream in which he saw rising from the earth a golden cross, which rose into the sky over where the monastery stood. When he awoke, he immediately roused the others and told them of his dream. His accomplices, believing what he told them to be an act of tomfoolery, laughed, at which point Uthlagus became angry and stated that the valley below was a holy place and one day men from all nations would go there on pilgrimage. Without further hesitation, Uthlagus packed his belongings and, kissing each of his criminal accomplices goodbye, he went down into the valley and lived out his remaining days in the carved out cave as a hermit. Thus it was that, by the middle of the 12th century, the area of Dale Abbey had received a holy reputation.

On many occasions, locals from the village have reported seeing the figure of a ghostly monk wandering around the Abbey. There are also reports of chanting being heard coming from the area where the Abbey would have stood. Frequent too are the reports of a hooded monk, which has been seen standing near the great chancel arch.

The hermit's cave is also known to be haunted by several ghosts. One local lady, while walking her dog in the vicinity of the cave one evening, distinctly heard crying noises coming from within the carved-out cave. On investigation, she found the cave to be completely empty. Her dog appeared quite apprehensive and, on turning to walk away, she distinctly heard a male voice call out her name. So frightened was she

Dale Abbey Hermitage – the Hermit's Cave at Darley Abbey is said to be the haunt of a figure of a ghostly monk who is believed to be Prior Henry. He was found to have been counterfeiting money and was also having a relationship with a working girl from Morley, in whose company he was embarrassingly discovered. He was subsequently arrested, but committed suicide by cutting his wrists while taking a hot bath.

by the experience that she now refuses to venture anywhere near the cave as she is convinced the site is haunted.

The ghost of the monk seen near the area is believed to be that of prior Henry, who, having taken his own life, is doomed to wander the face of the earth as guardian of the ruins until Judgement Day.

Dale Abbey was once a place of holy pilgrimage, as Uthlagus predicted, as it contained two holy relics: a piece of the Blessed Virgin Mary's girdle and a sacred phial containing some of her breast milk, both of which were said to have miraculous healing powers.

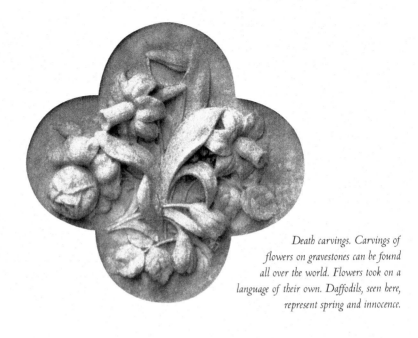

Death carvings. Carvings of flowers on gravestones can be found all over the world. Flowers took on a language of their own. Daffodils, seen here, represent spring and innocence.

The Language of Flowers

There was a time when man looked deeper into the meaning of all things that inhabited and grew upon the earth, and it was from the dawn of civilisation that man began to give particular attention to flowers. Their beauty must have stirred the imagination, eventually giving way to flowers being endowed and credited with magical and curative powers. Eventually, folklore naturally became interwoven with superstition, which in turn caused a vast amount of literature and legend to grow up and around the subject. This interest has continued to grow and there are now hundreds of books dedicated to the subject on the shelves of bookshops.

Flowers have many given meanings and over the centuries we have given certain flowers to one another in order to convey specific messages. They have been wreathed round the newborn baby's cradle, are carried by the bride and adorn the marriage altar, are sent to an admirer and are also left on the tomb.

The custom of dressing wells, predominantly associated with Derbyshire, is thought to have originated in Pagan times when mankind worshipped all spirits of nature, believing that all things – trees, rocks, plants as well as the clouds, winds and rain – harboured spirits. Dressing wells is alleged to be the ancient form of worshipping the spirits of antiquity held within the life-giving waters. Tissington, in north Derbyshire, still holds the annual custom which can be traced back to the period of the Black Death in 1348–49. Approximately a third of England's population perished from the disease, yet some villages, such as Tissington, remained untouched. The local people attributed this to their pure water supply and, to show their thanks, they took to dressing the wells. Flowers, fruits, berries, leaves, twigs and pine cones have all been used in this ancient custom; they are pressed into slabs of wet clay to form a beautiful piece of artwork. The finished plaque is then placed before the well for all to admire.

It has been alleged (although it has not been proved) that the Black Death also inspired one of England's most famous nursery rhymes, *Ring-a-ring o'roses*. The 'ring around a rosie' supposedly referred to the red rash that is the first symptom of the disease. 'Ashes, ashes' or 'atishoo, atishoo' referred to the sneezing sound made by the person infected and the last line of the rhyme, 'we all fall down' represented the many deaths resulting from the disease.

Perhaps the most interesting line of this rhyme is the second, 'a pocket full of posies', which referred to the practice of carrying flowers in the belief that it would protect the infected person. Some flowers are still said to hold protective powers to those that carry or grow them. For example, some say that to carry a sprig of yarrow will provide protection from any negative forces, while others say that you must carry a sachet of peony flowers if you feel you are victim of the evil eye. There is also the belief that the foxglove, traditionally known as the flower of sorcery, will keep away all evil spirits.

In Victorian times, the subject of flower lore became extremely popular. Mediums of the day took to using the subject of flowers as a practical means to divine the future. This practice has continued to the present day and there are still those who claim the ability to divine future events from a flower or leaf an inquirer might pick. Indeed, whole services have been dedicated to the use of reading flowers. Individuals wanting to make contact with a dead relative or know of some future element in their lives need only pick or choose a flower. They would even take it along to a service and place it on a tray, normally where the medium cannot see it, and later have it analysed. At this point, the medium will try to discover which person picked or chose the flower. This may appear to be a dubious way of making contact with the spirit world, yet there are those who state they have witnessed astoundingly accurate results.

The Victorians also sent flowers as a means of communication. However, it was of utmost importance that those involved believed in the same meanings, as many flower dictionaries of the time contradicted each other, therefore causing many misunderstandings and arguments!

Carvings of flowers can be seen on many gravestones in Derbyshire churches, each perhaps conveying further messages about the deceased that words cannot express.

The following list of flowers, their divinatory and superstitious meanings, is perhaps one of the more common lists of interpretations to be found. For those wishing to study this ancient art, it is worth remembering that it is equally important to give the flower a meaning that is also apparent to you. To divine a flower's meaning by inner intuition is just as good as knowing and using its ancient interpretation.

Aster – One used in love divination. To burn an aster flower is said to drive away evil spirits and serpents. Sentiment.

Amaryllis – Pride and haughtiness.

Anemone – Sickness, forsaken and forlornness.

Bachelor's Button – Love and marriage.

Buttercup – The smell was once thought to cause insanity. Ungrateful and conceited.

Bluebell – Some say tragic loss, others state it is the flower of constant kindness.

Carnation – Said to have sprung from the tears of the Virgin Mary on her way to Calvary. A lucky flower.

Camomile – Hope in a hopeless situation.

Chrysánthemums – Love, truth and happiness.

Crocus – Youthful hope, an end of a troubled time.

Daffodil – Regard and chivalry. To find the first bloom growing denotes a year when you will have more gold than silver.

Bluebell gravestone. Each and every flower has its own meaning. Bluebells were considered to represent suicide and disaster and were considered one of the official flowers of the dead.

Dahlia – Instability and illness.

Daisy – Flower of the children. Innocence and sentiment.

Dandelion – Courage and strength.

Dead leaves – Sadness, melancholy and a funeral.

Fern – Sincerity.

Forget-Me-Not – True love remembered.

Foxglove – Keeps away evil spirits and was traditionally known as the flower of sorcery.

Flowering fruit – Prosperity, fertility, growth and abundance.

Geranium – Stupidity and folly, also the flower of treachery.

Goldenrod – Health, encouragement and good fortune.

Hollyhock – The flower of fruitfulness.

Honeysuckle – New love and friendship.

Hyacinth – Said to have sprung from the blood of a friend slain by the god Apollo. A flower of regeneration.

Grave fruit. Flowers and fruit were once believed to have magical and curative powers. These symbols became increasingly popular as grave carvings in Victorian times.

Iris – A message travels towards you. Guidance.

Ivy – New friends and acquaintances.

Jasmine – Grace and elegance. Divided love reunited.

Jonquil – An expression of desiring someone to love you.

Lavender – Long life. According to one legend, the lavender once did not have any scent. The Virgin Mary hung the clothes of the infant Jesus on the bush to dry, and from that day to this, the plant has been imbued with its magical scent. This legend gave rise to the ancient belief that lavender flowers keep away evil spirits.

Lilac – Unlucky to have in the house, a flower of humility.

Lily – Purity and sweetness. Folklore states that lilies, unplanted by human hand, would spontaneously appear on the graves of people executed for crimes they did not commit. It is also said that the use of lilies at funerals symbolises the restored innocence of the soul at death.

Lily of the Valley – The return of happiness.

Love in a Mist – Love at first sight.

Magnolia – A love of all things in nature.

Marigold – The flower of reincarnation. Also the flower of mourning.

Mimosa – Protection from all evil.

Myrtle – A new love.

Narcissus – Vanity and egotism.

Orange blossom – Chastity and purity. News of a wedding.

Pansy – Once considered an extremely magical plant. William Shakespeare confirmed its magical uses when he wrote how Oberon squeezed juice from the flower of the pansy into Titania's eyes as she slept so that, when she awoke, she would fall in love with the first person she saw.

Peony – The seeds were once used to place curses on people. The flower of shame.

Poppy – Remembrance and consolation.

Primrose – A new life awaits you.

Rhododendron – Caution, you are moving into danger.

Rose – Love and beauty.

Shamrock – Laughter and cheer.

Snapdragon – Presumption.

Snowdrops – Another flower which is said to have sprung from the tears of the Virgin Mary. A flower of kindness.

Sunflower – Adoration and pride.

Thistle – False friends and enemies.

Tuberose – Dangerous pleasures.

Tulip – Fame and fortune.

Violet – Faithfulness in love.

Wildflower – Fidelity in misfortune.

Zinnia – Remembrance of friends absent.

Saints Among Us

There was a time when man not only prayed to God but also to an array of saints who, if moved by the individual's pious request in prayer, would intervene and grant whatever the plea might be, or at least bring out an alternative, satisfactory solution to the problem.

The word saint, as we have come to understand it, is more widely used in the Christian sense, especially within the Catholic faith. Saints were given their canonised titles by popes, whereas Celtic saints achieved their grand titles by the popular veneration of the people of the day, much to the annoyance of the later Catholic Church.

Holy men and women have always played an important part in western religions, from pre-Christian times until the present day, although today they are not as widely idolised as they once were. Most saints were people who, after death, were formally recognised, especially by the Roman Catholic Church, as having attained by holy deeds while alive great veneration by the poor and desolate people of their time. They often led lives of total devotion to their faith and were frequently purported to heal the sick and the dying as well as perform other remarkable miracles.

Specific saints dealt with specific requests, so if a saint had died in childbirth (Saint Margaret) then ladies suffering from any health problems concerning pregnancy or childbirth would pray to her asking for help and intervention in the matter. Within the Catholic church votive candles are still burned to invoke the favour of the requested saint

By praying to specific saints it was believed that the saint would take intermediate action between God and man, thus helping the request within the prayer to be granted or answered more quickly.

and it is further believed by many that, in most cases, the saints' intervention between man and God gets the answer and solution that is needed.

The following list is a brief guide to some of the more frequently invoked saints and what patronage they represent. Anyone wishing to invoke the aid of a saint must simply burn a candle on three consecutive nights while praying for whatever they wish to happen.

St George – Patron Saint of England and for all those fighting a battle (AD303).

St Sebastian – Patron Saint against plague and pestilence (AD288).

St Roch – Patron Saint of those who languish in prison or who are trapped (AD27).

St Cosmo and St Damian – Patron Saints of medicine (AD301).

St Christopher – Patron Saint of travel (AD364).

St Nicholas of Myra – Patron Saint of Russia and of children (AD362).

St Catherine – Patron Saint of philosophy, science and of students (AD307).

St Barbara – Patron Saint of explosions including thunder and lightning (AD303).

St Ursula – Patron Saint of young women (uncertain).

St Phocas – Patron Saint of gardens and gardeners (AD303).

St Pantelion – Patron Saint of physicians (fourth century).

St Apollonia – Patron Saint against toothache and all diseases of the mouth (AD250).

St Cecilia – Patron Saint of music and musicians (AD280).

St Agatha – Patron Saint against all diseases of the breast and of fire (AD251).

St Lucia – Patron Saint against all diseases of the eyes (AD303).

St Alexis – Patron Saint of pilgrims and beggars (AD400).

St Blaise – Patron Saint of diseases of the throat and of wild animals (AD289).

St Martin – Patron Saint of penitent drunkards (AD397).

St Eloy – Patron Saint of goldsmiths, locksmiths and blacksmiths (AD659).

St Anthony – Patron Saint of anything lost (AD357).

St Leonard – Patron Saint of prisoners, captives and slaves (AD559).

St Jude – Patron Saint of all those who are without hope (first century).

Ghost Bomber

The wind blew mournfully across the moors. Michael had begun to wish that he had not ventured out for his usual weekly hike, a walk that he normally looked forward to with a great deal of relish. Walking was his escape, his way of mentally detoxing from a demanding career in computers. The moors were located just a few miles from where he lived. Being deep in thought he began to walk across a patch of moorland that he had crossed dozens of times in the past. The heather and blueberry bushes were dense on this particular stretch. It was one of his favourite parts of the moor. The ground was undulating, it rose and fell every three or four hundred yards.

Crossing the brow of the largest of the hillocks, Michael found himself staring at a crashed aeroplane. Shocked and temporarily unable to move due to the horror of what he saw, Michael could do little but stand and stare. Smoke rose from the broken pieces of the aeroplane and a torn-off wing and a broken tail lay some 40 or 50ft away from the main body. Grey and white clouds of smoke mushroomed into the air from the remains.

The scene, although shocking, appeared to Michael to be somewhat odd. Although he knew little about aeroplanes, he knew enough to realise that this crashed plane was not a modern one. It looked out of time, displaced. The need to stand and morbidly watch the crash scene was soon overtaken by the need to run and help whoever might have been flying the plane. The movement of what was obviously a wounded man lying to the front of the wrecked craft sent him rushing down the hillside, heart racing and adrenaline flowing. The fear of what might meet his eyes on arriving at the strewn wreckage flicked through his mind.

Approaching the wreck, Michael could see clearly that there was indeed a wounded man lying on the ground. Being a matter of several hundred yards away from the crash, he attempted to quicken his pace. Negotiating a particularly tricky and boggy part of the moor, his feet sinking into the dark, smelly loam, Michael momentarily lost his footing and fell sideways. Regaining his stance, he forged his way forward. The wind appeared to have suddenly changed direction and the great wafts of smoke, which had previously moved due east of the plane, now began to move towards him. Within seconds huge blankets of the stuff engulfed him. It reminded him of being a Boy Scout and campfires at summer camp – how it always appeared that smoke inevitably would find you no matter where you sat or stood.

Knowing that the direction he had been heading in was still correct, he moved forward, grim determination now overtaking him and the urgency of the situation making him feel sick.

Arriving at where he thought the plane should be Michael found nothing. The smoke was still thick and visibility was still 10 to 20ft. Calling out into the smoke he received no reply, but he continued calling. Maybe if he could get to the injured pilot he might be able to administer some first aid. The desperateness of the situation was driving him to look harder. Peering into the haze revealed nothing.

It was at this point that the smoke began to clear. At first it seemed hardly noticeable, but then suddenly it cleared completely. There, before him, was a greater shock as he reached the brow of the hill. In front of him was nothing but empty space. Everything looked normal, everything as it should be. Total and utter

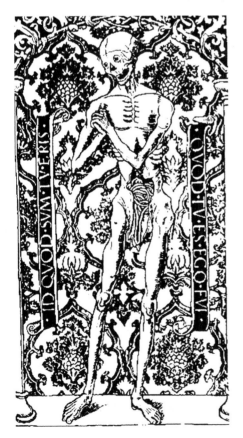

astonishment struck him. It was too much for his mind to handle at this point and Michael felt his stomach churn.

Such stories of phantom crashes and mysterious four-engined ghost planes spotted across Derbyshire and the Peak District are not uncommon. Ghostly sightings of Lancaster bombers and German aeroplanes are on the increase. One such hotspot for sightings of this kind is the Ladybower Reservoir, where it is reported that on moonlit nights a phantom bomber plane can be seen gliding silently over the still waters. One lady reported seeing a phantom bomber actually ascending from the waters of the reservoir and rising into the air. Other sites include Derby, Ashbourne and Glossop.

Dozens of planes were shot down or crashed during World War Two. It is the ghosts of some of the men killed in these crashes that are reported to re-enact their deaths. Many of the spots where the crashes took place are also said to be haunted; numerous people have reported seeing strange flashes of light, and hearing grinding metal noises and terrible cries of agony, as if an awful crash had taken place. On further investigation all searches revealed nothing in the vicinity.

One such site at Mickleover is said to have an annual reappearance of such a crash. Indeed, one lady living close to the field where the crash allegedly took place states that she is so used to hearing strange noises coming from the field that she often turns over and goes to sleep. 'But many a night,' says Pauline, 'I have found myself out in the field in my nightdress with a torch in my hand, looking for something untoward.'

Such sightings will probably continue to take place. Who knows why these spirits continue to haunt these spots? Perhaps it is their way of reminding us that war is often futile and the toll on life is great. Perhaps these active spirits are still not at rest because of the terrible way in which they departed this world.

Swarkestone Bridge:
The Army of the Dead, The Fighting Cavaliers
The Charming Brewhouse

Swarkestone Bridge is almost a mile in length and crosses an area of low-lying marshy land as well as the River Trent. It was originally built in the early 13th century on behalf of two beautiful sisters of the Bellamont family in memory of their fiancés, as legend has it.

The sisters were holding a party to celebrate their joint betrothal when the two young men were summoned to attend a meeting of barons on the other side of the Trent. They reached the meeting safely, but, while they were there, the river became swollen by a rainstorm. Although it became a flood of rushing water, the men were eager to get back to their beautiful sweethearts and attempted to ford the river on horseback. Their horses swam valiantly against the torrent but their efforts were in vain. Both men were swept away and drowned.

The heartbroken Bellamont girls built the bridge over the Trent to prevent such a tragedy occurring again, and in memory of the drowned men. Neither girl ever married. In fact, the legend states that they spent so much money on the bridge that they died not only unwed, but also in extreme poverty – being buried in one grave in Prestwold Church in Leicestershire. Their ghosts are said to be seen on stormy nights when the River Trent is swollen, looking for their lost loves who were so tragically drowned in the river's murky waters.

When Charles Edward Stuart and his small army of Highlanders reached Derby on 4 December 1745, one of their most important tasks was to send a party the seven miles from Derby to Swarkestone to try to secure the bridge over the River Trent. Swarkestone Bridge is the longest stone bridge in England, and in 1745 it was the only bridge across the River Trent between Burton and Nottingham. For the prince's army, it was also the only way to London and probable victory.

Seventy Highland soldiers, probably cavalry, were sent to secure the bridge and they reached it four hours before Government troops, who had been ordered to

Swarkestone Bridge. The macabre sound of Bonnie Prince Charlie's army can be heard marching across the bridge. Other ghosts that haunt the bridge are the Bellamont sisters still seeking their drowned lovers, who were tragically killed while crossing the flood plain.

destroy the bridge to stop Charlie's army from crossing it. Those 70 Scottish soldiers held Swarkestone Bridge until 6 December. Some of them went over it to Melbourne, to warn locals to prepare billets for the Highland army when they crossed over on their way to take the throne from King George II. This was not to be, of course, the decision being made at Derby to turn back. Thus, Swarkestone Bridge was the farthest point south reached by Bonnie Prince Charlie's troops.

Some 102 years earlier there had been a skirmish on Swarkestone Bridge between troops of Bonnie Prince Charlie's great-grandfather, Charles I, and those of Oliver Cromwell during the English Civil War. Sir John Harpur of Swarkestone fortified his own home and the bridge as well. Sir John Gell, the Parliamentary commandant of Derby, led his own regiment out of the town and hurled them against the Royalist barricades at Swarkestone Bridge. Seven or eight men were killed during that skirmish.

There have been many strange sightings at Swarkestone, one of the most interesting coming from a gentleman who told me: 'I was walking my dog. It was late at night and it had just started to rain when, in the distance, I could hear the sound of horses' hooves. I thought at the time that it was locals out for a late ride. This thought was soon dismissed as the noise of horses' hooves became accompanied by the sound of clatter and talking, which became louder and louder. My curiosity aroused, I waited in anticipation for the late riders to appear. They never did, although the noises became louder still, until, in the end when I thought that I could take it no more, the noise and the chaotic clatter stopped.

'My dog Harvey, with me all the time that the clamour was taking place, seemed not to have been affected by what had happened. Further along Swarkestone Bridge, I met a lady who also was walking her dogs and asked her if she had seen or heard anything. She looked at me blankly, stating that she did not know what I was talking about. I also asked two other people in the vicinity but they, likewise, denied hearing anything. Several months later, I was telling an elderly aunt about my experience. She did not seem unduly surprised and when I had finished she told me that she too had heard something similar in 1948. My aunt also told me that what I had experienced was apparently the ghosts of Bonnie Prince Charlie and his Highlanders trying to cross the bridge.'

Is it possible that this gentleman heard the ghosts of a cavalry detachment belonging to Bonnie Prince Charlie as they were being recalled back to Derby for the long retreat to Scotland and the eventual destruction of the Highland army at the Battle of Culloden?

Or could it have been the battling troops of Charles I and Cromwell's armies, re-enacting a skirmish on Swarkestone Bridge on 5 January 1643?

Not far from Swarkestone Bridge is the charming and charismatic John Thompson public house at Ingleby Lane, Ingleby, one of the few English pubs to have retained a wealth of charm and charisma. The John Thompson is famous for brewing its own beers. Brewing started in an outbuilding of the pub, which is a converted 15th-century farmhouse, in May 1977. A 12-barrel brewplant was installed. In the early 1990s a contract brewery called High Peak had their beers brewed here. In June 1998, Lichfield Brewery moved in to share the plant, with the two breweries using separate fermenting rooms. In early 2002 John Thompson started brewing their own beers again from the pub.

The building is said to be the haunt of several ghosts, but all of them are friendly. Anyone wishing to experience the atmosphere of a real old-fashioned English pub need go no further then the John Thompson, where the atmosphere is excellent.

On the lane outside the pub there have been reports of ghost soldiers seen silently marching; their skin ashen, they march with determined steps and as quickly as they appear they then mysteriously fade away into oblivion.

Other ghosts near to the pub include two fighting Cavaliers in full regalia. Seen on clear moonlit nights, their drawn swords glinting malevolently in the eerie moonlight, they fight to the death, backwards and forwards, forwards and backwards, until finally one is seen to pierce the other in his chest with his rapier before the two ghosts fade away.

The countryside that surrounds the John Thompson public house at Ingleby is some of the most beautiful around Derby. Anyone wishing to explore the ghostly folklore of such places as Anchor Church, The Seven Spouts Farm, Swarkestone Bridge and burial mounds, Melbourne, Repton and Foremark Reservoir can do so from this focal point.

Merry Spirits

Seymours Wine Bar

This wine bar and restaurant, which is tucked away in St Werburgh's Churchyard, behind the former church off Cheapside, is reputed to be the haunt of a figure of an old lady, dressed in grey. Several tales have been told regarding this lady, who has been sighted in the upper regions of the property. Members of staff stated that her presence was 'pre-announced' by the strong smell of lavender. Others reported that cutlery and other items were found to have been moved and some would disappear altogether, only to reappear at a later date. The area known as the Bake House was also described by staff as having a 'watchful presence'. Some even stated that they were touched by unseen hands, though they never felt that this invisible presence ever intended any harm.

Another interesting account was recalled by one lady and concerns the apparition of a young girl, who was seen in the upstairs bar...

'I had gone into Derby with a friend for a few drinks one evening and we went into Seymours. The bar downstairs was very busy so we decided to sit in the upstairs bar, which was empty. My friend wanted a pint of draught beer and, as the bar upstairs only kept bottles, he went back downstairs for the drinks, leaving me alone upstairs.

'I was sat at a small table in the corner, next to the open window as it was a very warm night and I wanted some fresh air. Suddenly, the air around me went very cold and the noises emanating from the busy bar downstairs became rapidly muffled. Although I didn't see anything to begin with, I distinctly felt the presence of someone stood next to me. As I turned to look once again, I felt the strong force of something move through my body. Subsequently, I saw the figure of a young girl who turned and smiled at me before looking out of the window. It was as if she had wanted to look out of the window and, because I was sitting in her way, she had to walk through me to get there!

'When the waiter arrived he asked me if I had just experienced something. I was surprised and when I asked him why he had enquired, he stated that the air around me was very cold and I looked as though I had been in some kind of trance. The bizarre thing was that I did not feel frightened in any way throughout the whole incident.'

The Bell Inn, Sadler Gate

The Bell Inn is one of the old coaching inns in Derby and has managed to retain much of its original appearance, although its apparent Tudor timbering was not added until after World War One. It was built around 1680, for the Meynell family, and is reputed to have various ghosts within.

A Victorian lady in blue stands in one of the downstairs bars and vaporises in front of staff and customers alike. A poltergeist in another downstairs room has been known to throw items around, one barmaid being hit on the back of her head by a wooden coat hanger, but close inspection of the room revealed no one else present.

Upstairs in the Bell, one of the rooms is haunted by the ghost of a serving girl who has been seen on frequent occasions, dressed in 18th-century clothing with a white mob cap. The original story, that she was murdered by the Jacobites in 1745, has nothing to substantiate it, but she has been seen on two occasions in connection with children. In the 1930s, the landlord had an asthmatic son. One afternoon he heard him coughing and choking in his bedroom. The boy's father ran upstairs and burst into the bedroom, to find a lady dressed in 18th-century costume bending his son over and patting him on the back. As the boy's father took over, the mysterious figure simply vanished before his eyes.

In the 1950s this same room was used as a nursery. One day the baby was being changed by the landlady and mother of the child. The mother moved away to get some nappy pins and cotton wool and as she turned back, standing over the baby and stooping as if to pick the child up, was the same figure in the 18th-century costume, complete with mob cap. The mother rushed to pick her child up and as she did, the ghostly figure completely faded away.

Perhaps the reason that this ghost lingers here is that she died trying to protect her child, or maybe even in childbirth. Perhaps she was not a servant at all, but a dedicated nursery maid.

The Dolphin Inn

This is Derby's oldest public house, dating back to around 1530. Of course, due to its great antiquity, it has various ghosts associated with it including a blue lady who walks through the old lath and plaster walls. She has been seen by many customers in the pub and also in the tea rooms upstairs. The most intriguing part of the Dolphin is its 18th-century extension on the left-hand side of the building in Full Street. This was not always part of the Dolphin, being originally a doctor's house.

In the 18th century, it was customary for doctors to have bodies delivered to their homes for the furtherance of medical science. Part of the sentence of execution in those days was that afterwards, the body of the criminal would be delivered to 'ye surgeons for dissection'. Many condemned prisoners were more fearful of the dissection then the death sentence.

Before the introduction of the new drop in around 1760, the victim was delivered to the hangman on a cart. The executioner then placed the halter around the victim's neck and the cart was driven away, leaving the condemned man swinging. It could take anything up to 20 minutes for the person to die of slow strangulation from the weight of their own body, unless, of course, the executioner happened to be feeling particularly generous. In this case he would climb to the top of the scaffold or tree, put both feet on the hanging person's shoulders and push down, or with his assistant they would take a leg each – this is where the saying 'pull the other leg' comes from – and pull down, thus tightening the rope around the neck and hastening the end.

Because of the length of time it sometimes took for the accused to die, some who were hanged and then delivered to the surgeons in the Shire Hall in St Mary's Gate woke up on the dissecting slab.

These poor wretches would be taken off and placed in a corner, where a careful eye was kept upon them to see if they would die or recover. A particular incident of this kind apparently happened in the cellar under the doctor's house, which is now part of the Dolphin.

The Dolphin Inn. Allegedly many ghosts haunt this pub, including a poltergeist that throws things around. Other strange things happen in the building, taps turn themselves on and off, things get moved around and crying has been heard.

One morning, so we are led to believe, our doctor came eagerly down into the cellar after a body had been delivered. He pulled the body on to a table and ripped the shroud from it, only to find life still present. No one knows what happened – whether the doctor died from shock, whether the person died, or if the doctor in fact plunged his scalpel into the body, or even if the person recovered – but many bodies were dissected in that cellar under the Dolphin, and to this day it is haunted by a poltergeist who turns the taps of the beer kegs off in that part of the cellar.

Because of the unearthly atmosphere two members of staff normally go down together, as no one wishes to venture there alone.

The Noah's Ark

One particularly industrious person who used the River Derwent in the 17th century was a gentleman by the name of Noah Bullock, who built an 'ark' and moored it on the Derwent near the Morledge. He lived on it with his wife, five daughters and four sons, whom he named Shem, Ham, Japhet and Benjamin. His religious devotion ended there, however, as Bullock's occupation aboard his floating home was the coining of counterfeit money.

In 1676 his crime – a capital offence in those days – was discovered and Bullock appeared before the Recorder of Derby, Sir Simon Degge, whom Noah knew well. The forger promised to end his activities, broke up his ark and sank it in the River Derwent, thus escaping the hangman. Today there is a public house in the Morledge bearing the name of Noah's Ark, a link with a notorious Derby character from the 17th century who is said to haunt the pub.

Close to the site where Noah Bullock may have built, moored and eventually sunk

The Morledge. The haunted Noah's Ark public house can be seen on the left. The area is said to be haunted by a coach and four horses as well as a man in a pinstripe suit seen holding a silver-handled cane.

Noah's Ark pub. Noah Bullock, the Derby counterfeiter, is said to haunt this building.

his ark, several river ghosts and strange lights which erratically move and twist in a strange dance have been seen. There is no explanation for these lights, apart from one medium who claims that they are the lost souls of the dead seeking a pathway to the next life.

The George Inn

The shrill sound of a post horn announced the arrival of the London to Manchester coach, as the tired horses picked up and flew through the streets of Derby. The large wheels clattered on the cobbles of the tiny road leading from Bold Lane to the George Inn in Iron Gate.

As the coach pulled up in the George Yard, off Sadler Gate, ostlers rushed out to hold the horses, and the coachman, wrapped in large overcoats one on top of the other, put away his whip and climbed down from the box.

Passengers going further had a little time for a meal in the coffee room. The George Yard was now as busy as a railway station at rush hour, with ostlers, coachmen and passengers going about the business of changing horses and getting the coach back on the road again within a quarter of an hour.

The George Inn was one of the most famous coaching inns in Derby and was built around 1693. By this time there was a distinction between inns and taverns, as inns were not only coaching houses, but also a place where gentlemen could stay if they did not own a townhouse in Derby. Many gentlemen certainly did stay at the George. The Duke of Devonshire frequented it on many occasions and during the 1745 Jacobite uprising he used it as his headquarters, holding the inaugural meetings which led to the formation of the regiment of soldiers called the Derby Blues.

In December 1745, the Blues held their first drill on the Holmes in Derby. They were dispatched to their billets and the duke and his officers went back to the George. At 7.30 that evening the news came that the Pretender's troops were at Ashbourne.

The Duke of Devonshire held a brief council of war in the George. Would the local troops attempt to prevent the Highlanders entering Derby? After all, wasn't that why they had been formed? But no, the duke marched out of the George, took his position in front of his troops on the Market Place and gave the order: 'The Derby Blues will retire'. Thus, they marched away towards Nottingham and left Derby to its fate.

The following morning two Highland officers rode into Derby. They inquired after the mayor but he had also left the town, so they hammered on the doors of the George and demanded billets for hundreds of troops.

Many other gentlemen stayed at the George during its long history. In 1763, Prince Viktor Freidrich Von Halt-Benburg stayed there for two nights. The George also played host to the Duke of York and Louis IX of Hesse, Darmstadt, in 1771.

Inns of the 18th and 19th century fulfilled many roles in the community, providing a place for courts, council meetings, recruiting offices and the buying and selling of animals. Doctors, dentists and vets held surgeries within the inns. In 1776, the George also took over as the post office while the one in Queen Street was being rebuilt. It also acted as a funeral parlour in 1773 when the body of Godfrey Heathcote, the Duke of Devonshire's comptroller, lay at the George en route for burial at Chesterfield.

The George, of course, has many ghosts and mysteries, none more bizarre than the George Skull. This female human skull, with a damaged cranium, was found by workmen 4ft down in a pit beneath the cellar floor. With it were animal skulls and bones, old shoes and strips of leather. Work was stopped and the skull was taken to Nottingham for forensic testing which showed that it was very old.

Now one's imagination can run riot. Perhaps this unfortunate female was murdered and thrown into a pit, or a midden – which would have been dug in earlier days. Animals would once have been killed on the premises to feed travellers and the unwanted parts thrown into a pit. Perhaps the woman was also thrown in there to conceal the murder.

Yet no other human remains were found, other than the skull. Perhaps she was not murdered. Perhaps those workmen digging in that cellar in 1992 came across something quite different, as the George stands almost on the corner of Iron Gate and Sadler Gate, the heart of Viking Derby. Gate is an old Danish word for street.

Iron Gate was where the blacksmiths traded and Sadler Gate was where the leather workers set up business.

Perhaps a Viking leather worker's shop on the site of the George was uncovered, which would account for the shoes and the discarded leather strips. The animal bones and skulls could have come from the animals killed for the leather makers. The hides would have been stripped and tanned and the off-cuts thrown into the pit.

Maybe the damage to the side of the skull was simply done by a spade because, in 1693, when the George was built, it was still customary to bury beneath the foundations of new buildings a human skull, a pair of shoes and a dead cat to ward off evil spirits and witches.

If that was the purpose for which this skull was buried then it has not done its job very well, as the George is decidedly haunted. On two occasions a long-haired man in a blue coat has been spotted walking along the landing in the middle of the night. He has been followed down the stairs into the bar where he disappeared, although there was apparently nowhere for him to go as the George was well secured. Also, crockery moves itself from the racks in the kitchen, but never breaks.

Since the refurbishment and extension of the cellar, bar staff have had strange experiences there: one found that stainless steel buckets were being thrown at him from a table and another, who went down to change the beer barrels on a Friday night, had to evade the plastic taps used on the beer kegs as they were hurled at him across the cellar floor.

A disembodied human groan has been heard in the cellar and on three occasions, in the presence of customers, thick pint pots have shattered, cutting the hands of barmaids and the landlady. There has been no explanation for any of the occurrences.

Ye Old Spa Inne, Abbey Street

In around 1773 a Dr Chauncey came across a mineral spring just off Abbey Street, Derby. Chauncey was an entrepreneur and seized the opportunity to rival places like Buxton and Bath. Simpson's *History of Derby* states: 'He put down a basin into the spring of it, to come out fresh: he built a cover over the spring which discharges itself by a grate and keeps the place always dry. About 20 yards below the spa he made a handsome cold bath and some rooms to it at considerable expense!'

Apparently Chauncey was only exploiting something which was already well-known. In 1611, the burgesses of Derby were already receiving rent for 'a watering place at the nether edge of Abbie Barne', so it appears that the commercial properties of the spring had been realised for at least 120 years before he decided to capitalise on them. Unfortunately, Dr Chauncey died in 1736 and his spa seems to have died with him.

A double-gabled cottage was built on the site of the spa. It then became a farm and, in the 19th century, a public house, which is what stands there today.

The buildings appear to be haunted, but whether by the ghost of Dr Chauncey no one seems to know. On frequent occasions the landlord has sensed that he is not alone in the cellars, and on three occasions his name has been called by a strange voice when there is no one else there.

Derby Silk Mill

England's first factory was built here in 1717, on the banks of the River Derwent. John Lombe, who was possibly the world's first industrial spy, travelled to Livorno in Italy to steal the patterns for making silk-throwing machines, spending his days working the machines and at night, when he should have been sleeping, copying down their plans. These he carefully placed in bales of silk destined for England. The plans were then intercepted by his father's agents and brought to Derby.

The silk-throwing machines were constructed in Derby's old Guildhall and eventually moved to what was the first purpose-built factory in England. Lombe escaped back home but three years later, so the story goes, he was poisoned by an

Derby Silk Mill. A young boy believed to have fallen to his death in the lift shaft is frequently seen here. Strange noises frequent the building and security guards have reported phantom figures seen on the stairs and upper regions of the building.

The Silk Mill pub. A ghostly cavalier in full regalia walks through the building and vanishes through a wall.

Italian assassin from Livorno, sent over to this country to exact revenge.

The Silk Mill burned down in 1910, and all that was saved was the bell tower. It is this tower which is known to be haunted by a little boy, who was kicked down the stairs by one of the overseers for not working hard enough.

Children as young as seven were employed at the silk mill. They worked from 5am until 7pm. This little boy's cries can still be heard at the foot of the stairs where he bled to death. On many occasions, staff of what is now Derby's Industrial Museum have gone into the tower, thinking that there is a child lost, but there is never anyone there. The lift operates by itself, often going up and down on its own. The museum staff check at night before leaving to make sure that no one is in the lift, as it operates so often in this manner.

Not far from Derby Silk Mill is a traditional English public house called the Silk Mill, the haunt of a Cavalier who is seen walking through a room known as the snug and vanishes through the wall. He is dressed in full Cavalier regalia including a sword and feathered hat. Clocks have been seen to jump off the wall and a strange smell pervades the bar area at certain times of the day. Several séances have been carried out in the building, apparently with some astonishing results.

Wraith of Shades

Interpreting Orbs: The New Wave of Spirit Photography

At the end of the 20th century reports of strange, often colourful, ghostly orbs being caught on camera began to emerge from all over the world. This new form of spirit photography coincided with the advent of telephone cameras and new digital photography techniques which were being eagerly embraced by a hungry market of creatively adventurous people. People who were delighted that they no longer needed to take a picture in the traditional way, but could digitally take a picture, plug the camera into their laptop or computer and have it up and in front of them, processed and printed within minutes of the picture being taken. Gone were the days of sending away your roll of film and waiting a week or two before the pictures were processed at a lab, returned and then collected.

It was at this point that a new phenomenon began to occur. Strange lights, mostly spherical, appeared on thousands of pictures! But what were they? Stories soon began to circulate about these often colourful orbs being the captured image of spirits.

For centuries mystics had claimed to be able to see auras and spirits, which they further claimed would appear to them in the form of spherical lights of differing sizes, density and colours. Was this absolute proof that spirits did actually exist and could even be photographed? No? Well maybe. No one has the answer. For those that believe no explanation is needed and for those that do not, no amount of proof will ever be enough. So, what are these strange orbs found on digital pictures? Flecks of dust perhaps trapped on the lens? Minute particles of metals suspended in the atmosphere of a room that, when photographed with a digital camera, reflect light in such a way as to appear like an orb of light? Or survival of the dead appearing on ever increasing sensitive technology. One thing is for sure, this new wave of spirit photography is here to stay, until such a time it can be finally explained one way or another.

The following colours and their meanings are what psychics and mystics use in deciphering what the orbs and the auras that they see around people mean. The colour is an indication of what the spirit was like in personality when they were alive. Likewise, the colours that often appear in blotches around people in photographs are an indication of their temperament and personality, or at the very least are a clue to their mood at the time the picture was taken.

Red

The colour of energy, passion, anger and love (depending on density). The best colour to be found in an orb or the aura is rose red, the colour of universal love and inner beauty.

Yellow

The colour of the intellectual and of clear thought processes. Orbs that display yellow are said to have been optimists, pleasant and had a balanced outlook on life in general, although their intellectual capacities in life were often under-stimulated if the colour dominates the orb or aura.

Blue

The colour of peace and beauty. Deep blue within the aura or an orb can indicate a strong emotional constitution and is said to indicate stability as well as long life. Blue is also the colour of healing. Electric blue will indicate spiritual awareness and latent psychic ability – mediums and psychics are often said to display this colour within their auras.

Violet

The colour of the highest vibration of light. Said to be stimulating, it is the colour of creativity and spirituality. It is not the colour for the masses but is found more often in the auras of spiritually developed individuals who care little or none for material possessions. Guardian angels are said to appear as a violet orb.

Silver

This shows energy and a strong will. Orbs with this colour are said to have been adventurous in life and would have sampled all aspects of living. People with this colour in their aura are often ideas people.

Grey

When found in the aura it will indicate illness, mental depression and lack of sensitivity. When found in an orb it is an indication that when alive this spirit was an ignorant, calculated and crude individual with an inability to adjust to life's ever-changing pattern.

Orange

This will indicate vitality, or lack of it, if the colour is found to be dark and murky. This colour often appears in the aura when the individual is in the process of recovery, be it spiritually, mentally or emotionally. When in an orb, it is an indication of an individual who was optimistic, kind, energetic and understanding.

Green

Harmony and balance, nursing and nurturing, and care and kindness manifests itself in the colour green in the aura and as an orb. Green will also indicate an individual's ability to communicate, although a dark and dirty green is an indication of an evil disposition; people and orbs who display this colour cannot be trusted.

Indigo

This is often the colour of nervous energy, mental and psychic forces, although too much of this colour within the aura will indicate a highly suggestible and neurotic personality which will be given to outbursts of uncontrollable self-pity. Orbs who have this colour are spirits who are said to have been kind, good listeners and often took on the role of counselling.

Gold

This will indicate a materialistic attitude towards life when found predominating the aura or an orb, although in small amounts gold will indicate a lack of self-esteem and a giving nature.

White

The colour of purity and goodness, kindness and compassion. Buddha's aura was said to be pure white and extend itself over one mile. Angels and higher evolved entities manifest themselves as white orbs.

Things That Go Bark In The Night

Since earliest times, man has revered certain species of animals for many reasons: some for their ability to live in harmony with humans, to love and in turn be loved, appreciated and cared for, and some for their innate ability to see the future.

Perhaps it is for these reasons – as well as for companionship and an obvious food source – that man decided to welcome all manner of creatures into the warmth of his home.

Many nations have worshipped animals, often in half-human form, as their gods and supernatural guardians, especially in Ancient Egypt, where all manner of creatures were worshipped, from the majestic lion to the fearsome jackal, humble beetle and bee. So revered were certain animals that, when they died, several weeks were often taken up in elaborate mourning and ceremonial embalming procedures before the creature was finally entombed amid much pomp and ceremony.

Native American Indians were familiar with animal telepathy; they believed they could communicate with all manner of creatures, especially wolves, which found great honour in the Indian totem. They gleaned much information from the wolves and watched their behaviour to define the weather.

Over recent years much research has gone into understanding the link between humans and their pets. One scientist has dedicated a whole lifetime to the study of animal telepathy, and, in investigating over 900 cases, one doctor claims to have discovered a definite link, which he describes as an invisible and 'morphic field' that exists between hundreds and thousands of pets and their owners.

For many years it has been believed that bees are telepathic and have a strong sense of what is happening to their keeper's family. It is common practice for beekeepers to inform the hive of any major events such as births, marriages and deaths, because if the bees are not told they will feel betrayed and abandon the hive. Bees are so in tune with their owners' lives that it has been known for them to attend their beekeeper's funeral.

The bond between pet and owner is said to be so strong that when something happens to one, the other immediately senses it. For many people, this will not seem unusual or bizarre; stories of telepathic occurrences are often told by ordinary, down-to-earth people who have no axe to grind on the subject whatsoever.

One lady, Dorothy Johnson, formerly of Little Eaton, stated that there is such a strong bond between herself and her dog, Terry, that she could not live without it. Dorothy often has to go into hospital for short periods of time. Her body gives her no warning of an attack, but some hours before she is taken ill her beloved boxer dog takes to jumping on her lap and whining in a pitiful way, something he does not normally do. It wasn't until the third time this happened that Dorothy realised Terry must have been trying to tell her something, that he could sense her health was about to take a turn for the worse.

Since she realised this, Dorothy's dog has warned her twice and, on both occasions, she has prepared herself for an attack and by doing so she has, as far as she is concerned, averted a greater disaster.

One more heartbreaking story is that of David Scarsdale, who lived alone with his dog, Jem, in Chester Green. Jem was a great companion to retired David and he would often talk to him, telling him of his daily troubles and arthritic pains. David felt that Jem would communicate in return, often coming to sit by his side when he was suffering or feeling sad, and not leaving him alone.

David frequently visited his daughter and her family, who lived in Somerset, although he would leave Jem in the care of his neighbour as his grandson had an allergy to dog fur. David's visits were usually only for a weekend, but at other times he would spend four or five days away. However, no matter how long the visit, his neighbour would inform David on his return that Jem would always know when he was about to return home. Jem would rush to the door and bark about 20 minutes before David's car arrived and could not be coaxed away from that spot until his master walked through the door.

On walks, David never needed to keep the obedient Jem on a lead; he would walk to heel wherever David went. However, one night it was raining particularly hard while David was out walking with Jem. For some unknown reason, and completely against character, Jem suddenly ran out into the road. A car was approaching and tried to brake, but because of the slippery surface, it skidded and hit Jem, who was immediately killed. David was distraught, feeling he had lost his companion and best friend.

A couple of nights after the accident, David was sitting alone watching television when he felt something brush against his legs. Feeling he had imagined it, he put it down to tiredness. However, the following afternoon when David returned from shopping, he found that his usually neatly-made bed had been disturbed, the covers had been turned back and there was a distinct impression made on the sheet as if something had been sleeping there, in the exact same spot that Jem used to lie next to David during the night.

Other strange incidents started to occur: David had mopped his kitchen floor one morning when he discovered wet paw-prints leading across the tiles to the pantry. The doors were locked so David knew that no animal had been able to enter the house. On another occasion, while David was away on his visit to Somerset, his neighbour had been into the house cleaning and was awaiting his return when she distinctly heard what sounded exactly like Jem's bark, a few minutes before David's car arrived.

David was never frightened by these incidents but instead felt comforted, believing that Jem was still with him, protecting and watching over him and the house.

There have been other stories concerning telepathic pets, including canaries, hamsters and even pet spiders. It would appear, however, that the majority of telepathic communications centre around our most common house pets – the cat and the dog.

Many people, just like David, are familiar with the feeling that their pets often know exactly what they are thinking; some owners have pets which sit by the telephone shortly before it rings, often with important news. One lady states that she used to ask her dog whether she should put her washing on the line or not, as she believed the dog could predict the weather; if the dog ran to the door, she could assume that the weather would remain fine, if he remained where he was, she knew that the weather was going to take a turn for the worse and her washing would be rained upon!

As in David's case, animals are also said to sense stress in their owners and relieve it by the process of being stroked. National magazines have often produced articles which claim that stroking our household pets not only relieves stress and anxiety, but is good for our health in general.

But why are animals so telepathic? Perhaps this is down to the fact that we are so advanced with technology and modern conditioning that we have forgotten how to use areas of our brains which most creatures, great and small, are still in touch with and continue to use. This phenomenon has now become known as Low Frequency Telepathy, LFT.

Headless Phantoms

Whatever stories abound concerning headless phantoms, the whole of the British Isles is strewn with tales of these decapitated wraiths. Several writers specialising in the supernatural have suggested that the primary reason for there being so many headless ghosts is perhaps due to the fact that, in times past, it was relatively common practice to decapitate the dead; this was done in the belief that it would put a stop to any spirits of warriors who were slain by Celtic head-hunters. Another school of thought maintains that these wraiths are the result of so many people being beheaded, from mediaeval times onwards, for political crimes against the monarchy. Archaeological excavations of numerous Pagan, Celtic and Saxon burials, have revealed that many of the remains of the interred corpses had been removed. Often the skulls were then placed between the knees or the feet.

Many of the headless phantoms that haunt the dark recesses of our world are male, although some can materialise as women, dogs and horses. Various ghosts either carry their dismembered heads under their arms, or are completely without a head, and the rare one or two have their heads placed on backwards.

Crossroads were sometimes considered magical places, as the four roads meeting formed the figure of a cross, which was universally accepted as a symbol of Christ, and therefore of protection. When it was thought that the dead person being buried may have been a witch, or in some way connected with the black arts, or

Satanism, then the corpse was often buried at a crossroads in the belief that this too would stop the dead from walking.

Every shire in the country appears to have their own individual headless phantoms. Many are seen on moonlit nights riding headless horses, while others are seen meandering through our valleys and villages in horse-drawn carriages, often carrying an empty coffin which is, according to most of the local legends, said to be for the unfortunate individual who meets the gruesome cortège.

As to where the missing heads from these decapitated phantoms are, many of our shires have been, at some point in time, abundant in screaming skulls. These curios which, for centuries, have been known to reside in many of our farms, or more often than not our manor houses, are thought to be a by-product of the headless phantoms.

Being notoriously spooky artefacts, these recalcitrant objects have been known to wreak havoc and mayhem if they are in any way moved or upset. Many famous accounts exist of screaming skulls being moved or, more often than not, thrown out of properties only to be reinstated later in their original positions. When the skulls have been removed, it is often common to hear that disaster occurred shortly afterwards to the residents of the farm or house. Farm animals often come down with mysterious diseases, while the owners, or even the individual responsible for the cleansing, are dogged by exceptionally bad luck or mishap.

Other areas of the world have equally interesting stories to tell of headless phantoms and ancient skulls. Perhaps the most famous accounts of strange skulls are the ones said to have originally come from mysterious temples, deep within the Mexican rainforests. These skulls, said to total 12, are carved from solid quartz crystal and are believed by many to have magical qualities. According to the legend of the crystal skulls, when the 12 are placed together it will signify the end of the world. In recent times, whole television programmes have been completely dedicated to the subject; the final findings concluded that the skulls were indeed of ancient origin and much of the workmanship which created the skulls is remarkable, considering they were alleged to have been created by such rustic people.

The Legend of Knowle Hill

Lady Johanne and the Severed Hand
The Monk that Finds No Rest
The Poacher and the Stone

Anchor Church is not a church at all but rather an ancient sandstone cave which, over the centuries, has been enlarged to include two rooms with windows. Standing on a section of the River Trent between Ingleby and Foremark, known as Black Pool, Anchor Church has a long history of being haunted by several spirits; one certain legend associated with the vicinity is a particularly tragic one.

According to an ancient document entitled *The Severed Hand of Johanne with the Long Hair: A Legend of Knowle Hill and Anchor Church*, there once existed a grand castle at Knowle Hills, near Ticknall, in about the middle of the 12th century. The castle

belonged to Sir Hugo and Lady Johanne Burdett who, having been matched in marriage by their parents, are said to have existed in total matrimonial bliss. So happy were the couple together that even the wife of King Henry II, Eleanor, is quoted as having frequently said to her husband 'There are few couples in your domain that set so good an example as Sir Hugo and his Lady Johanne'.

Stone head at Wirksworth Church. Mysterious and often inexplicable disembodied carved heads have been found across Derbyshire. The Celts were a race of people who worshipped heads, often decapitating their enemies in war and taking them back to their villages.

The couple lived happily for a time until an evil man known as Baron de Boyvill of Castleton – cousin to Sir Hugo – met and secretly lusted after the beautiful Lady Johanne. So intent was the baron on dividing the two that he set about persuading Sir Hugo to abandon his home, become a crusader, and join the growing numbers of knights who were responding to the call of the Holy War. Suspecting what the evil baron was plotting, Lady Johanne pleaded with her husband to stay in England, informing him that she was displeased with the effect Baron de Boyvill was having on him.

For a short while Johanne's plea appeared to work. Sir Hugo temporarily forgot about the Holy War and Johanne was content to go back to the way they were living before the arrival of Baron de Boyvill. However, not content to leave the loving couple alone and driven by his lust, Baron de Boyvill enlisted the help of a monk named Father Bernard, whom the evil baron encouraged to pay regular visits to a Monastery of Black Canons at Repton.

Sir Hugo was often in the habit of visiting Repton, frequently venturing near to the monastery gates, where monks arriving home from the Holy War would reiterate their tales of battles and bloodshed. Sir Hugo would listen eagerly to the stories and became increasingly downhearted at not being able to go to the Crusades, so downhearted that eventually he decided to seek spiritual guidance from a monk, Father Bernard, who by this time had made himself well acquainted with Sir Hugo.

Shortly after making the decision to seek guidance on the matter, Sir Hugo met with the friar who, having already been strongly primed by Baron de Boyvill, advised him that it was his duty to go to war and fight for England's cause, and furthermore it was almost certainly what God desired. Before leaving, Father Bernard handed over a sachet of powerful sleeping powders to Sir Hugo, advising him to administer the sleeping concoction to his wife the night before he left, lest she should weaken his resolve to go. Several weeks later Johanne awoke one morning from a troubled sleep to discover that her beloved husband had gone. Hanging around her neck was a gold locket with the words 'five years' inscribed upon it; her husband had left to join the Crusades!

On discovering that her husband had departed for the wars, Lady Johanne immediately became distraught; for three long years she is said to have existed in a state of depression and unhappiness, and to pass the lonely hours away she took to embroidering an altar cloth. The threads for the embroidery were said to have been made from her own beautiful long hair, which she mixed with strands of gold and silver, the pattern intricately depicting insects, birds, trees, fruits and flowers. When the altar cloth was finished Lady Johanne planned to place it on the altar of Our Lady of Repton, as an offering for her husband's safe return. However, all hopes for Sir Hugo's homecoming were shattered when news reached her, via Father Bernard, that he had been taken prisoner by the Turks, who were holding him to ransom.

Taking only a short while to gather all the gold necessary to secure her husband's release, Lady Johanne immediately dispatched the fortune with the monk. As the days passed into weeks and they in turn into months she became increasingly anxious, taking to sitting at her bedroom window and watching for any sign of Sir Hugo's return. A year passed by when, one morning, glancing from her window Lady Johanne saw an armed figure, upon horseback, riding up the avenue and into the courtyard. Upon the riders breast was the symbol of the red cross, sign of the crusades. Believing the figure to be that of her husband, she ran with open arms to greet him and discovered to her horror that it was none other then the evil Baron de Boyvill. Without hesitation the baron immediately began to tell Lady Johanne that all that had been handed over for the gold and silver she had sent was the dead body of her beloved Sir Hugo. Little sympathy was shown for the now heartbroken widow, and the baron informed her that, considering the fact that Sir Hugo had no heir, he was now the rightful owner of the castle and all the lands that went with it. Furthermore, he would allow her to stay on at the castle if she agreed to be his wife. Struck by absolute horror at his suggestions, Lady Johanne promptly and flatly refused, stating that she would take no other; as a result of this statement the baron imprisoned her in the castle for a period of five years.

When the period of her confinement had elapsed Johanne was informed that she was to become the baron's bride. The baron immediately left the castle to invite and collect guests for the marriage, a marriage that she knew she could not hold off any longer. Suddenly the door to her room was flung open and there, silhouetted in the doorway, was the husband she had thought she would never see again, Sir Hugo. As he entered the room, Johanne knew from his countenance and the expression upon his face that something was wrong, 'Unfaithful woman' he cried accusingly 'betrayer of thy husband, thy hour of punishment is at hand.' As soon as these words had been spoken, Sir Hugo drew his sword and, clasping the unfortunate Johanne by the arm, he struck a blow which severed her hand, adding the words 'This hand on which I placed a bridal ring shall be the sacrifice of thy infidelity, thus I immolate my revenge.' Turning away from where Lady Johanne lay bleeding to death, Sir Hugo marched from the room. Later that day Sir Hugo met with Baron de Boyvill, in the woods, where he was returning from the task of inviting guests to the wedding. A terrible battle is said to have taken place, the result being that Sir Hugo killed Baron de Boyvill and left him where he fell; later, his corpse was eaten by wolves, which were known to be numerous in the region at that time.

Many years passed by in which time Sir Hugo led the life of a recluse, never

Anchor Church exterior. The ghostly figure of a lady, believed to be Lady Johanne, is seen wandering along the banks of the river. Father Bernard still haunts this site, his spirit still not at rest for the terrible crimes he committed against the young lovers, Sir Hugo and Lady Johanne.

marrying again and very rarely venturing out of his castle. One dark and stormy night a messenger arrived asking to speak to the owner. Reluctantly, Sir Hugo granted him counsel. The messenger implored Sir Hugo to go with him to a cave nearby, known as Anchor Church, where an elderly monk, whose death was imminent, was asking to see Sir Hugo.

Anchor Church, Ticknall. The deceitful monk made his deathbed confession to Sir Hugo in this carved out room. Campers refuse to sleep here for fear of the ghost that mournfully cries just outside the window.

It was widely known that the monk at Anchor Church was a pious man who had chosen a segregated life of poverty and prayer. It was also rumoured that terrible screams of anguish, pain and cries of forgiveness could often be heard coming from the cave. So pious was the monk that he had received a reputation for being a miracle worker and pilgrims suffering from many maladies sought him out. Sir Hugo agreed to go with the messenger and, arriving at the cave, found the monk at the point of death. The monk immediately recognised Sir Hugo and, grasping his hand, begged him for his forgiveness, adding that it was he that had brought about the downfall of Lady Johanne. Once Sir Hugo had assured the monk of his forgiveness, the frail and clearly tormented figure reached beneath his robes and produced a parchmen, and no sooner had he handed the piece of paper over than he took his last breath. Unable to translate the contents of the letter, Sir Hugo hastened to Repton Monastery, where a monk read to him the following:

'The mendicant monk Friar Bernard and the recluse of the Trent are one and the same. Worldly vanity seduced me to crime – I wished to be thought a saint and I have been a wretched sinner. I travelled over Europe to gain partisans to the cause. I gathered money and spent it in wickedness instead of charity. The Baron of Boyvill paid me to gain over Sir Hugo de Burdett and I accompany'd both to the Holy Land. I betrayed Sir Hugo to the paynim's hands and after obtaining money for his ransom from his lady, I returned with the sum which I shared with the baron and found means to let Sir Hugo know that his lady was false and refused to ransom him. After this the baron came back to England and endeavoured by representing that her husband was dead to induce the Lady Johanne to become his wife, which she steadfastly refused. I had obtained large sums from the baron, but of late he had refused to give me more and in the end I wrought his ruin. I procured the release of Sir Hugo by my agents and sent him word that his wife and friend were both false. He encountered the baron in the woods of Foremark and slew him, for he taunted him with having gained the affections of his wife. Mad with jealousy, Sir Hugo put the innocent lady to death. Remorse almost drove me distracted when I found the effect of my work, and I strove by penitence to atone for my dreadful sins and those I had caused. Pray for my soul, and let masses be said for one otherwise lost forever.'

On hearing the words of the written confession Sir Hugo's heart filled with intense grief and, returning to his castle, he proceeded immediately to Johanne's room, which he had not entered since her death. There he discovered the inscribed gold locket, which he had placed around her neck before he had left for the Crusades, lying upon the embroidered altar cloth. He stayed in the room all night, clutching the locket and the cloth, bewailing his outcast state and asking God for forgiveness.

At sunrise, Sir Hugo wandered into the courtyard where the body of Lady Johanne had been interred and, kneeling by her grave, he made a solemn vow of everlasting love, adding that as long as life was held within his body he would take no other as his wife. No sooner were his words spoken than a nightingale, perched in a nearby tree, burst into beautiful song. Taking this to be a sign from God, Sir Hugo, according to legend, followed the bird until eventually he reached Ancote in Warwickshire and there built a monastery in expiation of his crime. Draped upon the altar of the new monastery was the exquisite embroidered cloth that the Lady Johanne had painstakingly made from her own hair. Thereafter, people with maladies of the hand would make a pilgrimage to the shrine of Lady Johanne, where many claimed to have received a miraculous cure for their afflictions.

Two ancient carved heads once existed at a farm near Repton, until a previous owner moved to another part of Derbyshire and is thought to have taken the heads with them. Seven Spouts Farm now occupies the site. I asked a local gentleman about the area and he replied 'I used to play on that site as a child, but now I would not stay in that place for any price. There is a stone in a field near the farm which, to this day, is stained with the blood of Lady Johanne and at certain times of the year blood oozes from it.' According to the ancient legend, there were originally three heads which were thought to have represented the three main characters in the legend of the Lady Johanne, for the ancient script concludes: '...and all that remains of the old building is now formed into a pleasure house – where usually not a sound is heard but the wind among the old trees and the rustle of the ivy waving to and fro along the old wall, where you see that strange face carved, that seems as if it were looking over the battlements watching what is going on. Some say on moonlit nights the whole figure has been seen and it looks like a knight in armour as it walks in stately step, all around this green where once stood a tower, and it pauses at a little doorway, utters a deep sigh and vanishes. There were two old women that once lived here and they used to hear and see strange things, chains rattling, and screams and groans that were awful. One of the old women died and used to come back to the other and tell wonderful secrets, so she said. But she went too, and nothing out of the common ever happens now.'

Today many people still believe Anchor Church and Knowle Hills to be haunted by the four main characters of this ancient legend. On moonlit nights it is said that a ghostly white hand can be seen gliding about by itself. One gentleman, who frequently camped at the site of Anchor Church as a youth, recalls how he was awakened one night by the sound of a man crying. Believing that it was his friend, who had accompanied him, and was having a bad dream, he threw an empty bottle at him to wake him up. The friend, without moving from his sleeping bag, answered 'It's not me!' Both froze with horror as they realised that the noise was actually coming from just outside the

Ghost monk. Carved out cave beneath Seven Spouts Farm, Knowle Hill. Eerie things happen here, one local stated 'You couldn't pay me enough to stay in that place.' The spirit of a malevolent monk guards the entrance to the cave.

cave. Neither dared go outside to investigate and for many minutes both sat there listening to the pitiful crying until eventually it just faded away. Even after the sounds of crying had gone the two sat there terrified that it might come back and, when the morning light broke the darkness of the night, they made haste to get away from the cave as quickly as possible. Other sightings of ghosts have taken place in the vicinity. Fishermen have reported seeing the ghostly apparition of a woman in white drifting along the riverbank.

Not far from Anchor Church and Knowle Hill is the Hangman's Stone, a stone with a deep groove set into it. According to legend a poacher rested there having first hunted down, and then killed and made off with, a deer. Feeling tired after the hunt he tied a rope about his neck and fastened the other end to his captured prize and went to sleep atop of the stone. While asleep the deer slipped off the stone to the opposite side of where he was sleeping and the poacher asphyxiated on his illegal booty. Many claim to have come face to face with the ghostly poacher, his face bloated and blue, and he pursues you through the woods making grunting noises. Others claim to have seen a hooded figure close to the stone, standing silently in solemnity. Ghostly sounds of people fighting and crying have also been heard. The most sighted ghost, however, is that of the monk Father Bernard; some say he is unable to find rest or peace for the terrible crime he committed against Lady Johanne, and that he is doomed to wander the area of Knowle Hill until Judgement Day.

In recent years there has been talk of Black Masses being acted out on the site. Other so-called witches are said to meet at the site and practice their dark arts. There are even reports that His Satanic Majesty visits the site on a regular basis. Especially at three o'clock in the morning which, according to ancient legend, is the hour of the Devil – the hour exactly opposite to the time which is universally believed to be the time of Christ's crucifixion. Many will not venture there after the sun has set for fear of meeting creatures not of this world!

Melbourne Church and Hall

In the 15th century, a castle existed at Melbourne and legend has it that Mary Queen of Scots was held prisoner at the castle in 1584, though she was quickly moved to South Wingfield Manor – the scene of the infamous Babington plot, which brought about her execution.

In the 17th century, the castle was allowed to fall into disrepair and all that remains of the building today is a wall. The stone, previously quarried from the area which is now the pond, was used to build Melbourne Hall. The house became the home of the Coke family in the early 17th century when Sir John Coke, Secretary of State to Charles I, converted the building using the stones from the old Melbourne castle. He was the founding father of the Melbourne Hall we see today.

Sir John's great-grandson Sir Thomas Coke, who lived at the hall from 1696, altered the house, giving it the east façade and before that the gardens, which are still arguably some of the finest of their style remaining in England. One of the most interesting features of the garden, and perhaps its most famous, is the unique

Melbourne Pool. Said to be bottomless, 'The Devil's Gateway' is the also the haunt of Caroline Ponsonby. A nearby cottage was the haunt of a terrible poltergeist for several years.

Melbourne Church interior. Fantastical carvings can be found within the church. Other strange carvings include several pentagrams, an ancient symbol adopted by witches.

arbour, which was designed and built by Robert Bakewell. The feature is known locally as the birdcage and is said to be the haunt of the tragic figure of Caroline Ponsonby.

Sir Thomas Coke's grandson, William, inherited the title of Viscount Melbourne on the death of his elder brother and later went on to become Queen Victoria's first Prime Minister. When the Queen gave her name to the Australian state, she named the capital after her faithful Prime Minister.

At the age of 21, William met and fell in love with Caroline Ponsonby, who was just 14 years old at the time. Four years later, the couple were married. They were known to live a happy life to begin with but Caroline, suffering from mental illness, was rumoured to have had several affairs – one such liaison was with Lord Byron. Caroline later went completely insane and eventually died in 1823.

Caroline's ghostly figure, dressed in white, is said to haunt the area around the hall before sweeping across the neatly laid out lawns and borders, passing near the pool and vanishing into the birdcage. Local legend states that the apparition also used to haunt some stone steps near to the pool. So frequent were her visits that eventually the gardeners at the hall were instructed to remove them in the hope that this would

Melbourne Church exterior. A spiritual seat since ancient times, the exterior of the church is the haunt of a 'White Lady' seen wandering between the church and Melbourne Hall.

lay the ghost. Apparently, this worked, as she is now seen only around the arbour. Others argue that the steps were not removed but were simply washed away during a flood, at which point Caroline's ghost moved itself to the area she haunts today.

In 1122, Henry I founded the Bishopric of Carlisle and one of its first ever endowments was Melbourne Church. Carlisle, being so close to the borders of England and Scotland, made it a prime target for raids by the Scots. Tired of the continuous raids, the Bishops of Carlisle retired to Derbyshire and this is one of the reasons why they built the magnificent church that we see at Melbourne today.

The Church of St Michael was built between 1133 and 1229; the large size of the church is due to the bishops still needing to carry out their duties when Carlisle was being raided. The Bishops of Carlisle held residence at Melbourne for nearly 500 years.

The Norman parish church is outstanding in the respect that it has been little altered since its construction over eight and a half centuries ago. The building is home to many interesting and unusual features. The massive drum pillars, 15ft high and 4ft in diameter, have many carvings scratched into them. Some are simply stonemasons' marks, yet others appear to be pentagrams, the symbol of which can be traced back to Pagan worship.

The church is still home to the Parish Chest, which was once used to store the church silver and to keep books safe. Near to this wooden chest is an interesting wall painting – a depiction of the Devil with two women kneeling beneath him. The picture is thought to depict man's greed and is a warning against avariciousness. However, some occultists believe that the painting represents two witches offering his Satanic Majesty what appears to be a holy host or some kind of sphere, possibly a magic looking-glass. The picture may well indeed be a warning against vanity, or a reminder that those who would dabble in the dark arts would go to hell. Witchcraft was certainly common at the time this picture was painted.

There are also carvings of several animals, including a grinning cat, a snarling dog and an ostrich. One final interesting carving is that of a Sheila-na-Gig, a Pagan representation of a fertility spirit who was said to preside over all the needs of man.

The Church of St Michael is reputed to be the haunt of a white lady. She is said to have been seen wandering between Melbourne Hall and the church, and has also been seen inside the building, standing near the altar. She is described as being young,

The Grinning Cat. This strange carving on the interior of Melbourne church shows a cat grinning. Cats were once worshipped because they were considered to have magical powers. Here in England the cat was approached with apprehension as they were believed to be half in, half out, of heaven and hell.

Melbourne Church Devil. This very early painting shows a picture of the Devil, or a demon, with two women kneeling beneath him, or are they worshiping him? The picture is thought to represent greed or vanity and is a warning against avariciousness.

perhaps in her twenties, and is wearing long, flowing garments. Witnesses have described her as being a 'peaceful spirit', who never seems to intend any harm. She simply stands unmoving next to the altar before fading before their eyes.

Other ghosts to be found in the area include a hanging man seen swaying to and fro from a tree close to Melbourne Pool, but when you go to investigate he has vanished. The pool itself is said to be bottomless and an entrance to hell that the Devil frequently uses. Several houses in Melbourne are haunted, with at least two of them being the regular haunt of a poltergeist.

Don't Look Back

Elvaston Castle and Churchyard

One of the many stately homes in Derbyshire that has remained preserved is Elvaston Castle, which lies five miles south-east of Derby. Designed by James Wyatt and built in around 1817 for the third Earl of Harrington, Elvaston Castle has been a popular country park since 1970. The site dates back as far as Viking times and was then known as Elvostune, after the Viking named Elvo.

The present building contains a wing that dates back to the 16th century and it is from a bay window of this older part of the building that the figure of a lady, dressed in white, has been seen moving from side to side, as if she is seated in a rocking chair. Workers at the castle have reported seeing her making her way from room to room accompanied by the sound of banging doors, as if she is displeased.

No one is sure whether the ghost of this lady belongs to the castle or to the surrounding grounds as she has also been seen in the churchyard. The church dates back to the 13th century, although it is possible that another existed there before the present one was built. Many people have seen the white lady accompanied by a large

Elvaston Castle, haunt of numerous ghosts. The window, shown here, is the only surviving piece of the original building. The ghostly figure of the 'White Lady' has been seen at this window on numerous occasions.

white dog, not unlike a wolf hound, in the grounds of the castle. One local legend states that she was the daughter of an earl, and that she died of a broken heart because her betrothed had been killed during a war.

Within the churchyard, half hidden beneath an enclosure of trees, lies a grave, the stone inscribed with the following:

In

Remembrance of
Hannah, lamented Daughter
OF
Samuel & Elizabeth Jordan
OF THIS PARISH,
WHO DIED NOVEMBER 18TH 1854.
Aged 22 Years.
My fragrant, blooming flower hath droop'd & fallen
A base deceiver with his hellish acts
And lying tongue, my peace hath slain
And all my family o'erwhelmed with grief.
With love's sweet name upon his demon lips
With banns & promises & flattering tales
Her confidence he gained, her ruin seal'd,
Seduc'd, betray'd; her tender heart was broke
Her body to an early tomb consign'd;
Her loving soul to realms of blifs has fled.

B. Berresford, Belper.

Another theory is that the white lady is the ghost of Kathleen Emily Harrington, wife of the 9th Earl of Harrington. Her grave does not lie within the Harrington family crypt, but instead

The grave of Hannah Jordan. The tormented soul of this unhappy wraith is said to haunt the vicinity of the churchyard and castle.

Elvaston summer house steps. The steps adjacent to the summer house where the figure of another white lady is often seen, as well as a procession of lights seen coming down the steps.

Elvaston Castle summer house. The mysterious summer house in the grounds of Elvaston Castle. It is here on dark nights that the phantom figure of a terrifying dog can be seen. Strange music is also said to come from the building.

lies on the other side of the graveyard. Perhaps the white lady apparition is that of Kathleen Harrington, not at rest because she has been estranged from her husband and the rest of the Harrington family?

Another ghostly tale told of Elvaston Castle concerns the Happy Huntsman's tree, which is situated adjacent to the grave of Kathleen Harrington and has a small plaque at the foot of the tree bearing this title. One of the Earls of Harrington was killed in a hunting accident in 1917 and left strict instructions within his will that his beloved hounds should continue to be let out to hunt on Boxing Day each year. However, when Christmas came and the Earl's instructions were carried out, the hounds simply ran around the Happy Huntsman's tree, refusing to move anywhere else despite efforts from the huntsmen. It is therefore said that the tree is haunted by the ghost of the Earl of Harrington.

Elvaston epitaph. A terrible curse carved in stone. Such horrid words, such terrible anger, is there any wonder that the spirit of Hannah Jordan can find no peace?

The County Gaol
Student Halls of Residence, Agard Street

In between Vernon Street and South Street, just outside Derby city centre, is the home of the former County Gaol, which opened in 1827 and was the site of Derby's last public execution in 1862. The condemned man was 26-year-old Richard Thorley, who was accused of murdering his former lover, Eliza Morrow.

The murder took place on Agard Street, a few streets away from the gaol, on 13 February 1862. Charles Wibberley, who was 10 years old at the time, observed the killing and his testimony later provided crucial evidence in Thorley's trial. Charles saw the couple arguing before Thorley produced a cut-throat razor and lunged at Eliza.

Doctor Joseph German, a local surgeon, was summoned to the scene but the lacerations on Eliza's neck and face were so severe he was unable to save her life.

Thorley's relationship with Eliza Morrow seemed to have been an unstable and somewhat aggressive one; the two were reported to argue frequently and their disagreements sometimes became violent. Eventually, Eliza (seemingly tired of her stormy relationship with Thorley) started to court a soldier. Thorley was extremely jealous about this relationship and began stalking Eliza, asking her to give up her new liaison. It seems that, in his confrontation with his former lover, Thorley became so enraged with jealously that it led him to murder her.

Thorley was apprehended by Detective Sergeant Vessey shortly after midnight on that fateful evening, and, when told he was being arrested for the murder of Eliza Morrow, Thorley replied, 'I have done it. I cannot help it now. I am sorry.'

Thorley faced trial on 24 March 1862 and, when the jury came quickly to their verdict of guilty, Thorley was sentenced to be executed by hanging at noon on 11 April 1862. It is estimated that between 10 and 15,000 people gathered to watch his execution. Thorley's body was left hanging for a full hour before being cut down and buried within the prison walls.

There are many ghost stories told by people from Derby concerning Thorley and the murdered Eliza; workers at a former factory on Agard Street were so familiar with both 'the lady in blue' and the 'phantom with the chains' that they referred to the two ghosts as 'Lizzy and Dick'.

Students from Derby University, living in the halls of residence on Agard Street, have reported hearing scratching sounds in the early hours of the morning. One young lady states that, on one such occasion, she awoke her friends in adjacent rooms to see if they could discover where the noises were coming from...

'We all congregated in the corridor and stood in silence, listening. The scratching sounds appeared to be coming from one of the bedrooms at the far end of the corridor, so we went to investigate. On entering the room, the noises stopped. We stood there for a few moments listening, before realising that the scratching had started again elsewhere. We returned to the corridor and listened again. This time, the noises seemed to be emanating from the opposite end of the corridor. However, when we went to investigate, the noises stopped. While we stood listening, the scratching started once again – strangely it seemed to be coming from the bedroom we first visited, now at the opposite end of the corridor! We found that, no matter which bedroom we went to look in, the noises started again elsewhere. It was incredibly frustrating, yet oddly spooky at the same time.'

Other executions took place at the gaol and, macabre as it might sound, public hangings were reported to be extremely popular, attracting thousands of people at a time. In recent times however, the site has been very quiet – yet it is still home to its fair share of grisly tales. Some people state that, if you walk past the gaol alone at midnight, you are sure to hear the sounds of chains being rattled, accompanied by the sound of a distressed wailing.

Other members of the public, who reside in the blocks of flats behind the gaol, have reported some poltergeist-like activity taking place in their homes – doors slamming of their own accord, objects disappearing and later reappearing in a different location, problems with water systems and televisions turning themselves on and off. Perhaps these

Markeaton Brook. When the brook broke its banks and flooded, several inmates at the Friargate Gaol were drowned. The disturbing sounds of a baby crying can be heard here.

153

moments of paranormal activity are the result of the ghosts of the unhappy prisoners who were executed for their crimes over a century ago – their souls forced to remain trapped forever? Or, perhaps there are more logical explanations...

Touched by an Angel

The great chain of being is a classical western mediaeval conception of the order of the universe; it is a somewhat complicated hierarchical system composing of numerous links from the most basic elements – the rocks and the earth – to the highest perfection at the top of the chain – God. Everything has its own assigned place within the chain, giving order and meaning to the universe.

Directly beneath God in the chain are the angels, who are subdivided into their own ranks: archangels, seraphim, cherubim, thrones and several others. It is said that there are seven angels that stand before the throne of God: Gabriel, Fanuel, Michael, Uriel, Raphael, Israel and Uzziel.

It seems that man has always believed in the existence of angelic beings, which mediate between the realms of mortals and the immortal gods, bearing messages of great spiritual importance, guiding the hand of man and silently watching in the

wings. Only in recent times would it appear that angels are physically and more frequently changing the fate of certain desperate and needy individuals.

In the Judeo-Christian culture, the word 'angels' signifies their work as messengers – other words denote their essence. To many these celestial beings are known as sons of God, ministers, servants, watchers, the holy ones. To others they are known as spirits and heavenly hosts. In Psalms they are

Triumphant angel. Do angels guard and guide us? Can they intervene in our hour of need? Many people believe in guardian angels, many further claim that they are frequently visited by them.

referred to as 'the chariots of God', while in the book of Job they are called 'morning stars'.

Every culture appears to have its own interpretation of what an angel might be, the descriptions often being remarkably similar. Ancient references to angels describe them as being without wings, residing close to man, so close in fact that the sons of God had intercourse with the beautiful 'daughters of men', producing a race of people known as Nephilim. It was only later, in 600BC, that angels and archangels appeared to move to a higher spiritual sphere, seemingly too pure by this time to reside so close to mankind.

Most Westerners, when they hear the word 'angel', automatically think of Christianity and the images they describe are reminiscent of the depictions of angels in Christian art — beautiful, winged human forms. Many believe that angels are entirely of Christian or Judaic origin. In truth, they are encountered in Hinduism, Shamanism, Buddhism, Taoism, Zoroastrianism and Islam among others. Angels were also frequently found in Paganism; you only have to look at mediaeval churches to see thinly-disguised Pagan gods in the form of angels: Hermes, Victory, Earth Mother, Eros, Pan and many more.

Modern-day individuals who study angels (angelologists) insist that we would not recognise an angel even if we stood next to one. They also state that angels and other such supernatural spiritual custodians are drawn to an individual through need and not want.

Many people claim that we all have a guardian angel which watches over us, intervening only when we need them to — often without us realising it.

One such story is told by a Derby lady, Laura, who, having experienced great loss and torment, decided to end her life...

'I had recently lost my daughter to a particularly aggressive and incurable form of cancer and, having taken so much time off work looking after her, I was also made redundant from work. I was struggling financially, in deep grief and really did not know which way to turn. Things really started to get on top of me and I decided that I simply could not go on.

'It was a few days before Christmas and I had been walking in a trance around the city centre, when I wandered up to St Mary's bridge. It was snowing really hard and no one else was about as I stepped nearer to the edge of the bridge and looked into the dark, cold waters below.

'I shut my eyes, muttered a silent prayer asking for forgiveness and prepared to step off the edge. Suddenly I felt a hand grab my arm. I was shocked and, when I opened my eyes, I looked into the kind face of a tall, handsome gentleman. "Go home", he said to me gently, "your son has visited you unexpectedly with great news and is waiting for you."

'Despite the cold weather, I suddenly felt enveloped in a cocoon of warmth and began to feel horrified at what I had almost done. As I stepped away from the edge of the bridge, lost in my own thoughts, I felt I should thank the stranger for his kind words. As I looked up however, he was nowhere to be seen. The snow had settled on the ground and there were no other footprints around the area except my own.

'When I returned home, I found my son waiting for me, just as the gentleman had said. He had visited me with Christmas presents and with the news that I was going to become a grandmother.

'From that day onwards, my life took a turn for the better. I realised that I had much to live for; I grew in confidence and found myself a new job within a few weeks. Within the year I had managed to afford a bigger home, closer to my son and my new-born granddaughter. I truly believe that the mysterious gentleman I encountered was an angel, sent to me in my hour of need.'

Such supernatural occurrences are not as uncommon as we might imagine. Indeed, all across Derbyshire, reports of angelic intervention in ordinary people's lives is on the increase. A stranger who helps an old lady across a busy road, the woman with medical knowledge who happens to be present when a man has a heart attack, the man who helps at the scene of a roadside accident before vanishing into the crowd, and any stranger who just happens to appear at the exact moment when help is needed. All these individuals, being of natural or supernatural origins, can be deemed angels. As to any real evidence of their existence, we have only the mysterious messages that occasionally appear in personal columns of newspapers, thanking a stranger who has helped another stranger in distress. These communications are perhaps the only signs that angels leave behind.

We can explain away most claims of angelic manifestations as natural occurrences, but not all. Indeed, many sightings may be due to over-active imaginations, others caused by sheer tiredness, while some may even be mild hallucinations caused by a myriad of different things. There still remain, however, those which we cannot explain.

There is a current belief that angels manifest themselves to us in the form of white feathers. These feathers mysteriously appear when we least expect to see them. There are accounts of people being comforted by the discovery of a feather, believing it to show that their guardian angel is with them. An interesting story comes from Mason Kennedy, who recounts the following...

'I was very close to my father and when he was diagnosed with an incurable illness I was gutted and didn't know how I would cope without him. I was 14 years old and he knew I was terrified of being without him and would say to me "dunna worry lad, you'll be alreet, al be with ya, watching over your shoulder like a guardian angel". Within a few months he had passed away.

'On the day of his funeral I got up and went to put my suit on and there, lying on my suit, was a white feather. I dismissed it as a coincidence and continued to get myself ready. Later at the church, during the service, my eyes were full of tears and I looked up in an effort to push them back when I noticed a small white feather, seemingly come from nowhere, float down from the ceiling and land directly on my father's coffin. I felt comforted and the vicar, who had also noticed the feather, commented on the fact that angels can often show themselves to us in forms of white feathers.

'During the actual burial and while prayers were being said, I noticed movement out of the corner of my eye; to my amazement another white feather blew across the grass and went directly into the grave. By this time I was convinced that,

Angel at Uttoxeter Road Cemetery. Angels are said to come to us in many forms. Finding a white feather is believed by many to show that our guardian angel is watching over us.

Foremark Reservoir. Since the reservoir was created strange phenomena have been reported here. Many ghosts haunt this site, and unidentified flying objects are regularly seen here.

true to his word, my father was indeed with me. Now whenever I am feeling down or unhappy, I can virtually guarantee that I will come across a white feather, often in the most unlikely of places, and I know that my father is my guardian angel and is watching over me.'

Foremark Reservoir

Foremark Reservoir is located in the heart of the National Forest between Derby and Burton upon Trent.

Built in the 1970s, Foremark Reservoir draws water from the River Dove at Eggington, supplying Melbourne water treatment works. The reservoir holds 2,900 million gallons (13,200 megalitres) of water, with a surface area of 230 acres (93 hectares).

Foremark Reservoir is a wildlife habitat offering many outdoor and leisure activities, such as adventure playgrounds, fishing, bird watching, sailing and cycling, as well as countryside walks for those who want to explore and discover the magic of the growing National Forest.

Surrounded by woodlands, the site has many well marked trails for walkers and picnic areas, together with a small information centre and play area.

Several ghosts haunt the vicinity, namely that of a grey man who is seen wandering near to the edge of the water. A goblin is believed to abide in one particular part of woodland. He is described as being black in colour and accompanied by the vile stench of sulphur.

Strange lights have been seen weaving in and out of the woods, as well as skimming over the waters. One couple claim to have spotted an Unidentified Flying Object (UFO), which they pursued for some distance around the reservoir before it shot off vertically at an amazing speed. They described the object as being triangular in shape with three greenish lights beneath it. Other strange sightings of UFOs have been reported in the area.

Gargoyles

The word 'gargoyle' comes from the Latin 'gurgulio' and the Old French 'gargouille', both words not only meaning throat, but relating to the gurgling sound made by the rainwater as it ran through the gargoyle figure.

Gargoyles are carvings on the outside of buildings and were originally designed as a drainage system to direct water away from the walls, thus preventing damage and deterioration. Some of the earliest known forms can be traced back to the time of the Ancient Greeks, when they were fashioned out of terracotta. Later, wooden carvings emerged before carvings of stone became popular, reaching the height of fashion in the Gothic period. As

Gargoyles were placed on churches to ward off evil influences or satanic attack. In this picture, are the carved people afraid of the terrible gargoyle? Or are they frightened of something more terrible that might be standing in front of it? It appears that the gargoyle is protecting them.

time progressed, more and more imaginatively-decorated carvings appeared, including representations of animals, beasts and demonic spirits as well as people – many of which were humorous and are referred to more commonly as 'grotesques'. After the introduction of the lead drainpipe in the 16th century, gargoyles primarily served a decorative function.

Superstition held that gargoyles frightened away evil spirits, as well as carrying out their practical function. Many parishioners believed that the gargoyles adorning their church not only warded off evil spirits, keeping purity within their place of worship, but also acted as a reminder of the perils of evil, hopefully encouraging the non-believers to change their ways and join them for worship.

Many of these grotesquely-carved figures adorn churches across Derbyshire. Whole legends have sprung up concerning certain gargoyles; it is perhaps no coincidence that these same stories have direct relevance to the fact that the churches stand on ancient Pagan sites adopted by the Christian church.

Alan Taylor, who was raised in Derby and has remained in the city for the past 55 years, recounts the following…

'My father would often tell me stories when I was a child of "flying gargoyles" which would come alive at night, leaving their positions at the church, to fly around the village in order to protect people from evil when they were asleep and at their most vulnerable. I thought his intention was to frighten me and my older brothers in the hope that we wouldn't become wayward teenagers and wander the streets after sunset. I never believed that the stories he told stemmed from local legend, or that any of them had an ounce of truth in them, until I had an experience that I can only describe as other-worldly one night when out walking home alone.

Gargoyle. Originally used as drainage systems for excess water on churches the name gargoyle refers to the gurgling noises the water makes as it makes its journey down the guttering and through mouth of the carved creature.

'I was in my late 20s and had recently moved into a house on North Street, near the Five Lamps Area just outside the city centre. I had been out for the evening for a few drinks with some friends who had been visiting for the day. As we said our goodbyes, they offered me a lift home, but I declined as it was still warm outside and I was quite happy to walk home. In those days, cities were much safer to walk alone in at night and I thought nothing of an after-midnight stroll. I was walking along Queen Street when I caught a movement of something out of the corner of my eye, flying high above me. It seemed too big for a bat and, being dark grey in colour, I

Gargoyle, Market Place. Carvings like this one were once placed on buildings in an attempt to confuse, or even frighten away, evil spirits.

knew it couldn't be an owl. I stood still and watched the mysterious creature circle in the air a few times before swooping down and landing on the pavement about 20 yards in front of me. Not daring to move towards it, I strained my eyes to try and get the animal in clearer focus. To my increasing horror, I realised that I was surveying something that I can only describe as being gargoyle-like in appearance. The face was leathery, the set of its eyes were hollow and unblinking and the mouth agape with fanged teeth. The eagle-like wings remained half spread as the creature turned to face me full on. Suddenly and without warning the figure sprang upwards, extending its wings as it did so, and flew off into the sky so quickly that I could not see which direction it had taken.

'I ran home and was still shaken by the occurrence as I got into bed. I told nobody of my experience as I thought I would be ridiculed or called insane, but the following afternoon I revisited the area to see if there were any statues or other stonework on the street. I was hoping to find some logical explanation for what I had witnessed the night before and be able to put it all down to my over-active imagination. To my dismay there was nothing I could see that vaguely represented the creature I had seen. On my way back home I walked past St Michael's Church, my thoughts full of the stories of gargoyles my father had told me as a child. As I looked up at the church, I saw that each corner of the tower held a gargoyle, one of which was a figure of an eagle and looked remarkably like the creature I had witnessed the night before.'

Uttoxeter Road Cemetery

Uttoxeter Road Cemetery, with about 3,000 graves and a total of between 6 and 8,000 burials, holds a vast amount of local history. Many notable local dignitaries are buried here, some of whose stories have been long forgotten.

The cemetery was opened in 1842, about 20 years after England's very first one at Burnhill Fields in London. The chapel of rest was demolished in the

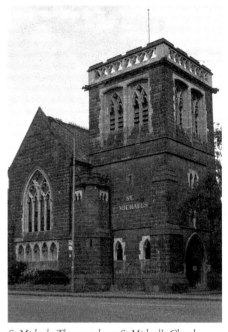

St Michaels. The gargoyles at St Michael's Church overlook the four cardinal points. The gargoyles seen here are a lion, an angel, an eagle and a bull, representing the four archangels; Matthew, Mark, Luke and John. Do gargoyles come alive at night and fly around the city? One late night reveller claims to have come face to face with one in the early hours of the morning.

1940s, probably because the cemetery was full and the chapel became little used. The area where the chapel once stood is now used for car parking.

Opposite the cemetery is an interesting building, dated 1851, to the designs of Henry Isaac Stevens of Derby. It was built as a diocesan training college and was extended between 1899 and 1913.

The old or general cemetery was opened in March 1843, containing four and a half acres 'tastefully laid out and fenced' at a cost of about £3,400. It was situated on the south side of Uttoxeter New Road, beyond the built-up area but easily accessible from the town.

A stone chapel, in the Gothic style, was built on the west side of the main entrance and a sexton's cottage was built on the east side, both buildings designed by Mr J. Hadfield.

Joseph Barlow Robinson (1821–1883), who worked as a stone carver for Pugin & Barry on the Palace of Westminster before returning to Derby to set up the Midland Sculptural & Monumental Works, was responsible for some of the monuments in the cemetery.

In July 1854, the cemetery was sold to the Derby Burial Board, formed in 1853, for £4,400. The Burial Board thus took over the management of both the old cemetery and the Nottingham Road cemetery. In 1895 management of the cemetery was transferred from the Burial Board to the Council of the Borough. The cemetery chapel was demolished in the mid to late 20th century. The cemetery is currently owned by Derby City Council.

Uttoxeter Road cemetery is said to be haunted by numerous ghosts: a man in a top hat and tails, a crying woman, a phantom dog, a vampire, angels that move their positions and a funeral carriage complete with two jet black horses seen in the vicinity of the sexton's cottage.

One young man reported having a strange experience when walking home late one night. While passing the cemetery, he saw movement out of the corner of his eye, coming from behind the iron railings at the top of the wall which surrounds the graveyard. This was suddenly followed by the feeling of something moving quickly about his head. So disturbed was he by his experience, that he did not linger to discover what it was, but ran home quickly!

Perhaps the most intriguing of stories comes from George Cobden, who once lived next to the cemetery. George recalls that soon after moving into his house, strange events began to take place.

For several weeks he would awake at 4am to the sound of eerie music emanating from the direction of the cemetery. On investigation he could find no apparent reason or explanation for the music.

Having woken him up, the music would last for approximately five more minutes before gradually fading in volume. As time went by, a female voice began to accompany the music.

Uttoxeter Road Cemetery angels. These angels at Uttoxeter Road Cemetery, the oldest cemetery in Derby, stand guard overlooking the graveyard. Some of the most prestigious and wealthy former residents of Derby are interred here.

George became tired from lack of sleep and decided to ask his neighbours about the strange music. None of his neighbours knew anything about it, and none of them had experienced being woken up in the early hours of the morning.

Then, one night, tired and irritable, he awoke to the now familiar sound of the music. Looking out of his bedroom window, which overlooked the cemetery, he could see light coming from one of the tombs. The light was 'bright and dazzling', and standing next to the grave were the figures of a man and woman 'dressed as though they were going to the opera or ballet'. George continued to watch the two figures for several minutes before the whole scene faded away.

The next day, George went into the cemetery and located the grave in question and demanded that those interred within, immediately stop waking him in the early hours of the morning with their music and singing. George was never woken at 4am again.

His Satanic Majesty
St Alkmund's Church, Duffield

St Alkmund's Church at Duffield is a fascinating little church with an interesting tale about its history concerning the Devil.

The church is dedicated to St Alkmund, an exiled Prince of Northumbria who was believed to have been murdered in AD800. Shortly after his death, he was made a saint and a martyr. The sarcophagus, discovered under St Alkmund's when the church was demolished in the late 1960s and believed to have once contained the remains of Alkmund, can currently be found in Derby Museum.

According to legend, St Alkmund's remains rested for a short while near a well. Thereafter, the water from the well was said to have miraculous healing powers. The well, known as St Alkmund's Well, still exists today and is said to be haunted by a monk, who is seen wandering around the vicinity dressed in a dark brown habit. This figure has also been seen on and near to Darley Playing Fields.

The church building contains

architecture of the 12th and 15th century. In the chapel is a fine alabaster tomb, dated 1536, upon which are the effigies of Sir Roger Mynors and his wife. Of particular interest is a wall monument dedicated to Anthony Bradshaw, his two wives and their 20 children.

Very few churches in England can lay claim to the fact that Satan himself chose the spot on which the church should be built, but Duffield church is one such building. According to an ancient legend, the site of the church was chosen to be near to where Duffield Castle once stood. The materials for the church were going to be partly provided by the remains of the old castle, which once belonged to the de Ferrers family who were at one time the Earls of Derby.

When work first began on the church, workmen arriving for a day's labour discovered that all their previous day's efforts had been undone and all the stone and building materials had been moved to a different location at the other end of the village.

This happened over and over again until, in the end, a priest was called to say prayers over the bricks and mortar. This failed and the building materials continued to move mysteriously.

St Alkmund's Sarcophagus. Now on show at Derby Museum and Art Gallery, St Alkmund's sarcophagus is said to have miraculous curative properties. People still take the waters from the well of St Alkmund in the hope of finding a cure for their illness'.

The former St Alkmund's Church, the final resting place of St Alkmund. The intricately carved sarcophagus was found beneath the foundations of this church, which was demolished in the late 1960s.

Finally, the workmen gave up and built the church on the site it still occupies today, by the side of the River Derwent; the site where the materials and stone were continuously moved.

From that time onwards, it was firmly believed by the people of the village that evil spirits occupied, or met at, the site where the church was originally intended to be built.

Tales of demons with red eyes and the regular appearance of the brown man were reported by locals. Very few people would venture there after sunset, for fear of meeting the arch-fiend.

Another version of the legend tells how His Satanic Majesty did not wish the church to inhabit an exalted position on the hillside, for fear that it would attract too much attention, and thus too many worshippers.

The ghost of the notorious highwayman, Richard 'Dick' Turpin, is said to haunt several sites in Derbyshire and the Peak District. At Duffield, he has been seen perched in a tree.

All the sightings of Dick have one thing in common: the phantom highwayman has no face and where eyes, nose and mouth should be, there is only an empty shadowed hole.

Lexicon Mystique

Animal Ghosts

Many paranormal investigators agree that animal ghosts do exist and believe that the spirits of animals survive the process of death. Elliot O'Donnell says in his book *Animal Ghosts* (1913) 'The mere fact that there are manifestations of dead people proves some kind of life after death for human beings, and happily the same proof is available with regard for a future life for animals; indeed there are as many animal phantoms as human – perhaps more'. Another school of thought believes that animals share a collective soul. This suggests that five, maybe more, animals at a time share one soul.

Apparition

An apparition is said to be the ghost of someone seeing something it recognises from life, or a ghost that appears in human shape looking and appearing as if alive. The tradition of apparitions goes back to the earliest of times and documented accounts litter the pages of history from pre-Roman times to the present. All world cultures and societies maintain accounts of apparitions. Some apparitions appear only when a disaster is about to occur, while there are also those reported to guard sacred places. Apparitions may not always be seen, but may be heard or felt.

Banshee

The banshee, or *'bean sí'* as this spirit should be correctly pronounced, is undoubtedly Ireland's most famous ghost form. Said to follow long-standing Irish families, she is more likely to be seen by the third daughter and is more commonly said to follow a family whose surname begins 'O'. Said to appear prior to the death of a family member, the announcement is made by crying and wailing during the night hours. The sound is described to be like a cat wailing but much worse. They are often described as being female and either a horrible old hag or else a beautiful young woman dressed in a green dress. A third type is ageless and has black holes in the place of eyes and nose. All three main types have long hair. In Scotland, a similar legendary spirit normally takes the form of a drummer boy or piper and likewise often foretells death or misfortune.

Barguest

One name for the phantom black dog. In appearance, the barguest is as large as a calf, with long sharp fangs and claws, fiery eyes and a shaggy black coat. The barguest seems to have been a name used relatively widely for a shapeshifting creature, which could also appear in the shape of a bear — indeed the name barguest may derive from the German for 'bear ghost'. In common with many supernatural creatures, the barguest could not cross running water and as a black dog it was often seen as a death portent.

Birds

There are many instances recorded of birds returning as ghosts. Birds were once believed to be messengers of the dead. When a bird tapped on a window, it was a ghostly spirit looking for another to join it. Some birds are believed to carry the souls of the dead into the afterlife.

Boggart

The name boggart is mainly used in Northern England and describes a particularly nasty type of ghost. Boggarts are said to have the habit of crawling into bedrooms at night, pinching, slapping and biting the unfortunate victims. They are described as being fearsome to behold, with sharp, yellowing teeth.

Bogie

Another rather unpleasant spirit, fond of haunting children, hence 'The bogie man will get you'. In British folklore, bogies are black in appearance with ugly grinning faces. Short and hairy with a foul smell, they were once thought to be the most powerful form of ghost, as they had once served the Devil. They often seem capable of wailing like banshees.

Brownies

A widespread name for a fairy or supernatural creature, they were small in appearance and wore brown-coloured clothing. Like many mischievous spirits they were thought to be attached to houses or families and could be helpful in menial household tasks. If offended they became malignant and mischievous, creating poltergeist activity and generally making a nuisance of themselves. To get rid of brownies all you had to do was leave them a new cloak and hood, and they would take it and never be seen again.

Cats

Next to dogs, cats are said to be the most common form of animal ghost. The ghost cat may have its origin in ancient Egypt, where the cat was worshipped. At Bubastis, thousands of mummified cats have been excavated. Historically, the Devil was believed to take the form of a cat. Likewise, the many ghostly and often black cats haunting many houses in England are sometimes thought of as being vice elementals, for example: spirits which have never inhabited any physical body and may have been generated by evil thoughts, or else attracted to a spot by some vicious crime or deed.

Changelings

It was once believed in Derbyshire that certain other-worldly creatures kidnapped newborn babies, particularly those of good appearance, and exchanged them with old, emaciated, decrepit and ugly fairy creatures who were known as changelings. The abducted children were not assumed dead but living in a timeless fairy place exiled from the mortal realm. Sometimes a lactating woman was also abducted to suckle these kidnapped mortals and sometimes to suckle fairy babies.

Church Grim

The guardian of old churchyards in the form of a black dog, the church grim protected the dead from the Devil, demons and other nefarious supernatural creatures. The dog was often seen on stormy nights and was regarded as a portent of death. It has been surmised that the church grim is a folk memory of a sacrifice. It was believed in the past that the first to be buried in a churchyard would have to watch over the rest of the dead. It is also believed that a dog may have been buried first in place of a human. Phantom black dogs are numerous in Britain, and almost every area has its own variant. Although not all of these are thought to be derived from a folk memory of a sacrifice, the practice was once widespread.

Clairaudient

The ability to hear disembodied voices of the dead or other entities; normally they will foretell events yet to happen. Many mediums claim the ability to hear the voices of dead relatives and then pass on this information from what they call the 'spirit world'.

Clairsentient

The ability to be able to feel things in a divinatory sense. Many mediums claim this ability is merely a refined basic human instinct.

Clairvoyant

The ability to see visions of events yet to happen, events happening in the present, or events that have already happened. Many mediums combine this ability with one or the other clairsenses.

Crossroad Ghosts

Crossroads have long been associated with hauntings and, although it is not exactly clear as to why, a number of theories have been put forward by way of explanation. Some consider it is as a result of a practice in older times for murderers, criminals and suicide victims to be buried at crossroads. This practice was said to confuse the spirit and prevent it from returning and haunting the living, the cross formed by the roads being used as a form of Christian protection. Witches were also believed to hold ceremonies and to practise their black arts at crossroads.

Dogs

Ghostly dogs are reported from all across the British Isles and vary widely in size. In Lancashire they have a black dog called Striker and in Wales there is Gwyllgi. Black dogs also frequent graveyards and desolate moorland and heath. Like the banshee, they may foretell death or misfortune within a family.

Doppelganger

The word is derived from German and is usually the expression for a ghost who is either still living or is an exact double of someone. Those who have experienced seeing their double are said to be heading for misfortune, and they rarely indicate good fortune. They are often experienced by friends or family of the person they are haunting, but in a place where the living counterpart was nowhere near.

Drude

This is an ancient English expression for a nightmare ghost, normally that of a mature witch — well versed in the arts of black magic. They are able to insert their ghost into the dreams and nightmares of their chosen victim.

Ectoplasm

This strange substance is said to be extruded from the sweat glands and body orifices of certain mediums while in a trance. The word 'ectoplasm', or 'teleplasm' as it is increasingly referred to, is derived from the Greek 'ektos' and 'plasma' – exterior substance. Described as being like pale or white silk strands or a jelly-like material, it is able to form human-like shapes. Some investigators have over the years claimed to have examined ectoplasm and stated it be biological in origin, but its present biology is unknown to man.

Elementals

These strange ghosts are said to be spirits which have never existed in physical form, unlike 'normal' ghosts and spirits which have at one time lived in a physical form, either human or animal. Occultists declare them to be ancient spirits which pre-date mankind and fall into four categories, comprising of earth, air, fire and water. Elementals are often associated with woodland, mountains or uninhabited valleys.

Exorcism

An exorcism is an act of religious ceremony used to expel a spirit, either from a human host or a building. The ceremony is normally performed by a specially trained clergyman who will often say prayers and repeat loud exhortations. The ceremony also involves burning candles or incense and the sprinkling of holy water. This is a modern version of the old Christian rite or excommunication known as the ritual of bell, book and candle. Modern mediums also claim to be able to perform a similar act, normally without the trappings of religion, by physically contacting the spirit and convincing it to move on to another plane of spiritual existence.

Extras

This widely-used term describes faces or sometimes whole images of people who appear mysteriously on photographs. Often the pictures show a white wispy substance out from which the face is normally starting to appear. In the early days of photography, many so called spirit photographs were produced, claiming to show the faces of the dead. Subsequently many, if not all, proved to be fraudulent. In recent years the white wispy form itself has appeared more and more, often without the attendant face. These are often described as vortex pictures, as a faint helix form is often to be discerned within the white cloud. Some researchers have declared them to be pictures of spirit energies.

Fairies

Fairies or faeries are said to be small, often invisible, creatures. They can provide great help or great hindrance to people. The colour green is sacred to them and they inhabit trees, hills and valleys. They are frequently also associated with ancient burial mounds or stone circles, and are similar in many respects to elementals.

Fairy Curses

If the fairy folk were particularly displeased with a person they cast a curse on him or her. The curses took many forms: the cows ran dry of milk or the milk was soured; the afflicted person became ill with a mystery disease which only a fairy doctor could cure; a cursed person became crippled with either a minor stroke, which only affected the face, or a major stroke which hit one side of the body. For major transgressions against the fairies, such as cutting into their mounds or cutting a fairy thorn, the penalty was death. In times past precautions were taken against the fairies. Salt and iron are two substances the fairies cannot withstand, so sprinkling the ground around your house with salt could protect you from them.

Fairy Fauna

There are many fairy trees along the roadsides and especially at the crossings of roads throughout England. Usually these are gnarled old hawthorn bushes. Also considered sacred to the fairies were the oak and the ash, while many magic wands were made from the rowan tree. It is considered a profanity to destroy them or even to remove one of their branches. Many different types of other-worldly creatures are said to dwell in the trees and plants of the fields and woods.

Fireball or Lightball

Frequently reported in haunted locations, the fireball or lightball is said to move in a slow and smooth manner. They are also frequently reported near to stretches of water. They are believed by some to be the souls of the departed returning to earth, in order to guide the souls of the newly departed to the next world.

Galley Beggar

This is an old English ghost, often reported in the North of England and mentioned as far back as 1584 in Reginald Scot's *The Discovery of Witchcraft*. This fearsome ghost is described as being almost without flesh and bearing its head under its arm and emitting a deathly scream. The name is derived from the word 'gallery', meaning to terrify. This ghost is likely to be encountered on country roads and deserted lanes.

Ghoul

From the common name for a ghost in Arabic, it is nowadays commonly used throughout the world to define a nasty or vicious-looking ghost. The ghoul is believed to gain sustenance from eating the flesh of corpses – hence a ghoul is often used to describe a ghost that haunts graveyards.

Goblins

Hobgobs, gobelins, hob-thrush, blobins, bogles, bogies, brags and boggarts. The word goblin is derived from the Greek 'kobalos', meaning rogue. The term goblin can apply either to the ugliest members of the fae, or to certain sub-races. Those fae numbered among the goblin sub-races include the Scottish trows, English spriggans, Welsh knockers, Cornish knockers, German kobolds and wichtlein, the Irish phooka and even Shakespeare's infamous Puck. They grow up to 30cm and are covered with a thick coat of black/grey hair. The goblin is usually found wearing very dark coloured clothes and a tall cap similar to that of the gnome. They can appear as animals.

Often portrayed as the villains and troublemakers of faerie, goblins are not truly completely evil. Though they seem to have no moral code of their own, they are happy to enforce that of their human hosts. The miserly and lazy are apt to feel their pinch, or find their rooms and possessions in disarray.

Goblins are pranksters and are known for rearranging items in the house, tangling horses, banging pots and pans, removing the clothes from sleeping humans, knocking on doors and walls and even digging up graves to scatter the bones around. Mine goblins make knocking noises by striking pickaxes and hammers against the stones. To placate a goblin one must leave out a bowl of gruel in the fireplace. When he has eaten he will help with any household chores that have been left unfinished.

Graveyard Ghosts

According to folklore, the first person to be buried in a churchyard was believed to return as a ghost to guard the site against the Devil. This ghost was supposed to have special abilities. Because the task was so great, a black dog or more rarely a cat was buried before any human so it would become the guardian of the dead. Ghouls are also associated with graveyard hauntings.

Gremlin

These have only appeared in recent times and the word is believed to have originated during World War Two, when pilots often reported strange goblin-like creatures in the aircraft with them. Gremlins were immortalised by Steven Spielberg in his highly entertaining film of the same name and today hardly a piece of machinery can go wrong without somebody blaming 'a gremlin in the works'.

Grey/Blue/Brown/Green/Red/White Ladies

Said to originate in Tudor times when the Dissolution of the Monasteries resulted in a great number of monks and nuns being made homeless. Nuns at that time were frequently habited in grey. Many other investigators subscribe to the theory that grey ladies are similar to white ladies, while others claim the colour is related to the surrounding substance – wood, plaster or stone – which may contribute to the ghost's appearance.

Hallowe'en

Originating long before the advent of Christianity, the Feast of the Dead is perhaps a better name for the night. It was a time of great celebration for our ancient ancestors, who would light great bonfires to try to summon and placate the dead. The Christian churches tried to mask the true meaning of the celebration by declaring it to be All Hallows Eve, the night before All Saints' day. Modern witches still celebrate the night of 31 October by the holding of feasts and the performance of rituals.

Haunted Chairs

There are many reported instances throughout England of owners who had a particular fondness for, or may have died in, an armchair – returning as a ghost and being seen in that particular chair. The ghost of Lord Combermere was reportedly photographed in his favourite chair, while his body was being interred nearby. Chairs also feature in many legends: chairs that cause death or misfortune to the sitter and chairs that result in the pregnancy of the female sitter.

Haunting

Used to describe a ghost or series of paranormal events which takes place on more than one occasion within the same building or at the same place, we refer to such a place as being haunted. Objects too can be haunted and subsequent owners may experience incidents that are paranormal. Haunted items include furniture, jewellery and even the bones of the deceased.

Headless Ghosts

These are believed to be the spirits of people who have died by being beheaded. Evidence also suggests that these types of apparition may be connected to the ancient practise of beheading corpses. Many graves have revealed burials with the decapitated head placed between the knees, perhaps in the belief that the dead would not come back to haunt the living.

Headless Horsemen

By tradition, this is the ghost of a rider who has been ambushed or decapitated when riding swiftly. Others believe them to be the figures of ancient chieftains who, having lost their heads in battle, still wander the earth seeking their lost heads. Headless coachmen are thought to be either the victims of highwaymen or perhaps were decapitated passing under archways or low obstacles.

Iron

This is thought to be a talisman against bad magic, witches and evil spirits. Used by many cultures in the past, Saxon burials frequently contain iron talismans to protect the spirit of the deceased during his journey into the afterlife.

Lemures

This is the Roman name for evil ghosts. The Romans believed that the spirits of the dead often returned to haunt relatives and friends. Ceremonies and rituals were frequently performed by many cultures to prevent such spirits returning.

Leprechauns

Leprechauns are the famed fairy creatures who own a crock of gold, which they usually bury beneath the end of a rainbow, or some equally ephemeral and difficult-to-find spot. They are shoemakers by trade and are usually found out of doors in rural areas. They are described as being no more than 2ft tall. It is said that if you can keep your gaze fixed on them long enough, they are compelled to lead you to their crock of gold, although they always manage to wrangle out of such compromising positions. Even if you do succeed in gaining the crock of gold, it usually turns to nothing more than dried up old leaves the following day.

They are noted for their fondness for alcohol, which is usually made from heather or gorse or other unusual herbs or cereals, the making of which is a lost art to ordinary mortals. They also have a great capacity to consume large amounts of ale and other intoxicating beverages.

Ley Lines

Ley lines or fairy paths are reputed to run throughout the length and breadth of Derbyshire. These mysterious underground lines of power are associated with magical, paranormal or unusual happenings. In some rural areas as late as the 1950s and 1960s people would consult a local dowser or wise man/woman to discover where it was safe to build their houses. There is even an instance of a house being torn down because one of its gable-ends was discovered to have been built over a fairy path.

Strange noises were heard throughout the house and the sounds of thousands of marching feet were heard in the downstairs bedroom on the north side of the house, which was the side that covered the fairy path. When the house was relocated a few yards south of its original location, all the disturbances stopped.

Materialisation
An ability claimed by some mediums to produce a visible spirit. One of the first recorded incidents of materialisation took place in America during 1860 by the Fox sisters, founders of modern spiritualism.

Mermaid Pools
Pools of doom, death pools or back water: these terms refer to many secluded ponds and lakes which are said to be haunted by a certain type of mischief-making ghost. Many people, when near them, report feelings of sadness and melancholy. Most of these pools also have legends of people being drowned and lost forever within their waters. The legends may extend back to ancient times when water deities were worshipped in many cultures, a practice that often involved human sacrifice – the body being thrown into the water.

Ouija Board

This consists normally of 38 figured cards arranged in a circle. The letters of the alphabet and the numbers zero to nine are represented, together with two further cards with the words 'yes' and 'no' upon them. Derived from the French and German words for 'yes', the board is thus correctly called the 'yes yes' board. It is alleged to act as a mediator between the worlds of the living and the dead. When using the board, a glass or pointer is used to indicate the letters and words being spelled out by the spirits. The board also carries with it a fearsome reputation for demonic possession to those using it, although in more enlightened modern times it is now believed to be a form of dowsing.

Phantom Coaches

The phantom coach is thought by many to be a messenger of death, similar in many respects to the banshee or phantom drummer boy. The coaches are always said to be black and the horses are usually headless, as may be the coachman. The driver or passengers are often skeletal or hideous, with fixed maniacal grins. Passing at great speed, it is frequently silent and, according to legend, anyone getting in its way will be carried off to their doom. This almost exactly tallies with the ancient Norse legend of the eternal hunt of their gods of the underworld.

Piskies

There are a number of creatures particular to Cornish folklore, although their cousins can be found elsewhere in Britain under a different name and guise. One of these strains is the piskie, also known as a pixie in other West Country counties. The piskie is a general name for a fairy race or tribe in Cornwall. In appearance they look like old men with wrinkled faces, and are small in stature with red hair. They dress in the colours of the earth, especially green, using natural materials such as moss, grass and lichen.

Generally, the piskies are seen as cheerful creatures with a prankish nature. They are said to be helpful but also mischievous, helping the elderly and infirm while sometimes leading the more able bodied traveller astray on the lonely moors. Many stories relate to travellers being led into the wild moorland to become hopelessly lost because of the piskies.

Poltergeist

The word derives from the German verb 'polter', which describes a noise caused by banging, knocking or throwing things around. Harry Price, in his 1945 book *Poltergeist over England,* describes them thus: 'A poltergeist is an alleged ghost, elemental, entity, agency with certain unpleasant characteristics, whereas our ordinary ghost is quiet, inoffensive, noiseless and rather benevolent'. In all lands and all ages the poltergeist is mischievous, destructive, noisy and erratic. A ghost is described as haunting whereas a poltergeist infests.

Psychic

This is known as pertaining to the soul and to the mind, being a mystic, clairvoyant or telepathic, or with the ability to be able to see into the future. This should not be confused with spiritual, which is often used these days to describe mediums who do not need to be psychic to be spiritual, but do need to be spiritual in order to be psychic.

Psychomancy

This is the ancient practised art of foretelling future events by the appearance of ghosts or spirits and what their manifestation means to the living.

Salt

Believed from ancient times to be like iron as a universal panacea against evil spirits and all manner of witchcraft and the Devil, salt is often used in rituals to subdue a ghost by being placed in all the corners of the haunted building.

Séance

These are normally conducted by a medium, who claims to be able to contact the deceased relatives or sometimes the spirit guides of the sitters. They sometimes involve materialisation, disembodied voices, or knocking and rapping sounds. The word séance is French in its origin and means a sitting.

Spectre

This was once used simply as another word for a ghost, but nowadays is more commonly used as a descriptor for a ghost, which is found to be explainable by hoax or natural occurrences.

Talisman

This is any object believed by the wearer or carrier to have the power to protect the owner from death or evil spirits. Talismans are also ascribed the power to bring good fortune, wealth or good health.

Telepathic

This is the ability to read minds and know the thoughts of other people, either close by or frequently at great distances.

The Goath Shee (Fairy Wind)

This was a deathly cold blast of air that you felt if you crossed over a fairy place, even in broad daylight on a warm summer's day. It could cause all sorts of malignities upon the unlucky person who felt it, most often one was hit with the stroke which left a person paralyzed. It was also known as the blast. Shakespeare refers to the blast in Macbeth when he writes:

> 'And pity, like a naked newborn babe
> Striding the blast, or heaven's cherubin horsed
> Upon the sightless couriers of the air,
> Shall blow the horrid deed in every eye,
> That tears shall drown the wind...'

(Act I, sc. 7, 21–25)

Trance

This is an altered state of consciousness described as being somewhere between sleep and wakefulness. In this state mediums claim to be able to use their bodies or minds as a channel for waiting spirits or even healing energies.

The Stray Sod

If anyone chanced to walk over some enchanted fairy ground they immediately lost their way, sometimes becoming lost in a familiar field. This piece of land was known as the stray sod, as it led you astray. Also, if any fairy beings had a mind to, they would also lead you astray and you had to follow wherever they led you against your own will.

Vengeful Spirits

There are many recorded instances of ghosts returning to avenge themselves of terrible wrongs which were done to them in life. The ghosts of Winnats Pass near to Castleton, in the Derbyshire peaks, are said to be the spirits of Alan and Clara, brutally murdered in the pass by a group of miners.

Wakes

This is an ancient custom, thought to originate in Ireland, of sitting and watching over the dead while consuming large amounts of alcohol. This tradition is thought to help the spirit of the deceased in their journey into the spirit world. The practice of watching the body is done to prevent the dead body being entered by an evil spirit. The noise of music, singing and dancing at wakes also helps to scare evil spirits away.

Warlock

This term is used wrongly by many writers to describe a male witch. Many such witches would find such a term insulting, as in times past the word also described a traitor.

Witch

This is a person, normally a woman, who practises witchcraft. There are many forms of witches. Most worship nature and call upon gods of fertility to help them with their undertakings. Witches are normally forbidden to tell anyone what they are or how they practise their art, believing silence is power and power brings knowledge. Modern witches would not use their powers to harm people, instead choosing to help and promote spiritual awareness and greater wisdom of life.

Wizard

This is a person, usually male, who is possessed with amazing abilities and is well-versed in the art of magic. Many male witches prefer this title to the perhaps more mundane warlock.

Wood Sprites

Wood sprites were the fairy elementals who lived in the trees and the woods. They were the protectors of the wood and were particularly fond of the oak, the ash and the hawthorn tree. These trees were considered sacred trees to the ancient Celts and were not tampered with. Even in modern times it is considered unlucky to cut down one of these fairy trees, as the spirit who dwells within will wreak revenge on the offending party.

Wraith

According to ancient tradition, a wraith is the ghost of a person on the verge of death and often appears as an exact likeness of their human counterpart. They are regarded as a death omen and should a person see a wraith of themselves, then their days are surely numbered.

Bibliography

Andrews, W. (ed.) *Bygone Derbyshire* (1892)

Anthony, Wayne *Haunted Derbyshire and the Peak District* (Breedon Books, 1997)

Barnatt, John *Stone Circles of the Peak* (Turnstone Books, 1978)

Bord, Janet and Colin *The Secret County* (Book Club Associates, 1976)

Brassington, Maurice *Roman Derby* (Breedon Books, 1991)

Daniel, Clarence *Derbyshire Traditions* (Dalesman, 1975)

Daniel, Clarence *Ghosts of Derbyshire* (Dalesman, 1973)

Daniel, Clarence *Haunted Derbyshire* (Dalesman, 1975)

Daniel, Clarence *The Story of Eyam Plague* (Blackwell & Wye Valley Press, 1983)

Elder, Isobel Hill *Celt, Druid and Culdee* (Covenant Publishing Co. Ltd, 1962)

Graham, J. McEwan *Haunted Churches of England* (1989)

Green, Andrew *Phantom Ladies* (1977)

Hippisley-Coxe, Anthony D. *Haunted Britain* (Hutchinson & Co. Ltd, 1973)

Jewitt, Llewellyn *Derbyshire Ballads* (London, 1867)

Litchfield, R.M. *Strange Tales of the Peak* (J. Hall & Sons, 1992)

McGregor, A.A. *The Ghost Book* (Robert Hale, 1955)

Mitchell, W.R. *The Haunts of Robin Hood* (1970)

Naylor, Peter J. *Celtic Derbyshire* (Hall, Derby, 1983)

Naylor, Peter J. *Manors and Families of Derbyshire, Vol 1 & 2* (Hall, Derby, 1984)

Pickford, Doug *Magic, Myth and Memories* (Sigma Leisure, 1993)

Power, E.G. *Hanged for a Sheep* (Scarthin Books, 1981)

Rhodes, Ebenezer *Peak Scenery* (1824)

Rickman, R. and G. Nown *Mysterious Derbyshire* (Dalesman, 1977)

Rogers, Frank *Curiosities of the Peak District* (Moorland, 1979)

Taylor, Philip *May the Lord Have Mercy on Your Soul* (Hall, Derby, 1989)

Toulson, Shirley *Exploring the Ancient Tracks and Mysteries of Mercia* (1980)

Turner, W.M. *Romances of the Peak* (London, 1901)

Underwood, Peter *The Ghost Hunters Guide* (Blandford Press, 1986)

The Peak District Companion (David and Charles, 1981)